SOUTHERN GREATS:

LESSONS OF LOVE AND LIFE LEARNED ON THE BLUFF

BY HOWARD WHITE

with CANDACE J. SEMIEN

SOUTHERN GREATS

Southern Greats: Lessons of Love and Life Learned from the Bluff
ISBN: 978-09908158-0-8

Copyright © 2014 by Howard White and Candace J. Semien

All rights reserved. No part of this publication may be reproduced, distributed, or transmitted in any form or by any means, including photocopying, recording, or other electronic or mechanical methods without written permission from the publisher, except in cases of brief quotations embodied in critical reviews and certain other noncommercial uses permitted by copyright law. For permission requests, write to southerngreats@gmail.com or to the address below:

TOP Choice
6960 Goya Ave
Baton Rouge, LA 70806

Ordering Information:
Quantity sales. Special discounts are available on quantity purchases by corporations, associations, and others. For details, contact the publisher at the address above.

Printed in the United States of America

ACKNOWLEDGMENTS

I would like thank my parents, Howard L. White Sr. and Edna M. White, who have always believed in me and in historically Black colleges and universities. When my dad said, "I will pay for you to go to Southern or Tuskegee, even though you have a full ride to other schools," I knew it was something special about HBCUs of which they are both graduates (Mississippi Valley State University and Alcorn State University).

This book is inspired by my late grandfather, John Allen White. He taught me many lessons that I am still discovering as true today.

To my son, Howard L. White III, for asking the questions and searching for 'why' in situations. Your future is as bright as you want.

To Southernites Monica Riley, James Brown Sr., and Mac Arthur Sholas. These individual gave me time, connected me to Southern Greats I did not know and pushed me to completion.

Thanks to Dr. Dennis Kimbro, who gave me time, advice and seven questions to consider as I was first starting this project, your life and work as an author, teacher, and mentor are priceless. Thanks for sharing.

To several mentors who I had when I was at Southern: the late Dr. Wesley C. McClure who always challenged me to be better; the late Donald C. Wade who taught me the importance of relationships; and Dean M.Q. Burrell who taught me to about balancing the various areas of my life.

To my pastor, Bishop Raymond W. Johnson of Living Faith Christian Center in Baton Rouge, for pushing me to seek excellence and fully utilize my gifts and talents.

To the team that help me to pull all of this together, Candace, Maya, Mary, and Byron, your listening and giving me unfiltered advice have been invaluable in my growth. I look forward to the future projects.

To the Jaguar Nation for supporting TOP Choice and more importantly for allowing me to be part of your world.

To my wife, Janice, for giving me the time and sacrificing the resources to make this project happen.

Most of all thanks for being the wind beneath my wings. Love YOU!!

METHODOLOGY

Southern Greats: Lessons Learned on the Bluff was first conceived during a road trip to Orlando, Florida, to prepare for the MEAC-SWAC Challenge in 2010. My son, Howard Lee White III, and I were driving through Tallahassee, Florida, when I decided to stop at Florida A&M University. During our drive through the campus, Lee had several questions about FAMU and who had attended.

As fate would have it, the Central Florida Chapter of the Southern University Alumni Association was having their monthly alumni meeting where I had the honor to meet and interact with one of Southern's highly accomplished alumnus, Mr. Irving Matthews. What was most impressive was not the businesses that he owned nor his home sitting on the Atlantic Ocean. What really impressed me was his love for Southern University, his story of accomplishment, and how Southern University was the bridge to help him achieve many of his accomplishments.

As I was driving back to Baton Rouge the next day, I begin to think about why more people don't know about Mr. Matthews. Then I started to wonder, how many more Irving Matthewses had Southern University produced and why won't someone locate them and share the story of these great alumni. The more I asked myself why this story has not been told, the more it became evident that I should locate these Greats—as many as I could—and share the story in the form of one compilation.

As an alumnus, it always amazes me how many fond memories that all graduates have when they speak of Old Southern, Dear Southern. There is always a sparkle in their eyes as they speak of their days spent on the Yard and in the bordering Scotlandville community.

Within the following 160 pages of *Southern Greats*, I have tried to capture some of those great stories and tales in a way that will motivate you to be the best person possible. However, the larger purpose remains to reach a little deeper, pull back the layers, and identify how Lady Southern can turn a country boy or girl from Smalltown, USA, into a polished gem ready to make major contributions to society. What is it about Southern University and A&M College in Baton Rouge, La., that enables it to bring young men and women together from meager and disjointed beginnings, receive them, educate them, nurture them, and produce men and women who the world must welcome and respect?

I believe that this is legacy that must be captured in various forms of media and we are starting the process by turning what answers we discovered into this book.

Here in *Southern Greats,* we explore and chronicle individuals who have been highly successful in their various professions. Anyone familiar with Southern University knows that Southernites have excelled in areas ranging from the military, Corporate America, education, sports, entrepreneurship, government, and humanitarian arenas. The list of individuals who I've included in this book is by no means meant to be all inclusive or totally comprehensive. The listing only reflects those alumni who were available and willing to be interviewed and talk candidly talk and speak about Southern. With their willingness and my unanswered questions, I began this work not knowing it would take nearly four years, two hundred hours of recorded interviews, 30,000 miles of travel, and two editors in order to complete this.

Today, I can proudly present to you *Southern Greats*, the alumni and the book.

TABLE OF CONTENTS

Acknowledgments 3
Methodology 5
The Beginning 10
Understanding the HBCU Experience 14
The Greats 20
Building Character 22
It's All About the Love 38
Refined by Mentors 52
Following Your True Passion 71
Being a Trendsetter...Being a trailblazer 95
Motivation and Self-Determination 111
Enjoying the Journey...Not Just the Destination 127
Always Bring Value 143
Conclusion 157
Southern Greats Interviewed 159
About the Authors 163

THE BEGINNING

The word 'beginning' is defined as "the point of time or space at which something starts." It is the first noticeable point of growth and development. The beginning is also the specific place where a framework or foundation is laid. It can even be the first point of change that later becomes a point of reference or the start of a memorable event. For many the beginning of something great, usually starts in the formative years of their lives.

To spend time reflecting on how successful people begin travelling the path of success requires that we research their formative years as well as the times in their lives where successful habits were developing.

For many people, thoughts about their formative years elicit powerful memories. The positive memories can motivate and fuel their desires to achieve and do more, while the negative memories can overtake and stifle any motivation to succeed. I've found that successful people habitually push aside and examine negative memories to find strength from them.

We often hear people complain and moan about their negative experiences. Some say things like, "I grew up broke and poor", "I didn't have my dad", "I didn't learn how to", "I wish I would have had", "We could not afford to", or "I wish I could have". These statements are not merely truth for them, but they are oftentimes excuses for not taking initiative, for not taking full responsibility, or for not working harder. The fact is that everyone has a backstory full of positive and negative memories. For us all, there are some particular incidents in our past that shapes—or even reshapes—our lives and gives us a new beginning toward who we will ultimately become. Within every experience, positive and negative, we find the characteristic traits of the whole person we will be. No matter your circumstance, surroundings, experiences, or background, there is always an opportunity to take the lessons from your formative years and come out stronger–and learn invaluable lessons in the end.

It is in the formative years where mentors, teachers, and advisors pour ideas and information into our conscious that will impact our lives. There are many people who contribute to us in such unique ways that help us determine how well we live our lives and how successful we become. These people are sometimes family, friends, teachers, neighbors, and even strangers.

I often reflect and draw strength from those early and formative years when I was young and just beginning.

Like most people, I took every opportunity to learn from the negative experiences and draw strength from the positive ones.

I think back to that time when I was just establishing my life's journey, wondering where my path would take me and what choices I would make while on that path. Every experience seemed to mark my beginning and each one inevitably determined my future. The circumstances that led me to attend Southern University and A&M College in Baton Rouge were a combination of academics and family tradition. My grandparents did not attend college, but they worked hard to ensure that my parents would benefit from a college education. My parents attended Alcorn State University and Mississippi Valley State University—rival historically Black universities in Mississippi. Starting early during my years in high school, Southern University played a significant role in my journey and became paramount in shaping my future.

While in high school, I had the honor of attending a six-week summer engineering program aimed at recruiting students into Southern's undergraduate engineering program. During that summer, I attended classes, lived in student housing, and completed various engineering projects. In the end, this academic experience solidified my decision to study at the Jaguar Nation. So, I did and majored in mechanical engineering. While there, I maintained several internships and relationships with mentors who helped guide me to matriculation.

> *Southern University is an institution that meets you exactly where you are, challenges you, nurtures you, and equips you to be successful in life and in your career.*

This is what draws and will continue to draw people from across the world to the Baton Rouge campus. It also holds true for all of the alumni—who I call "Southern Greats"—whose lives led them through the Baton Rouge campus and on to the road of success. The value that Southern University brings to its students is nearly indescribable. This book details the impact of Southern University on me and the forty-six Southern Greats you will read about in the upcoming chapters.

Understanding the HBCU Experience

With students and faculty from diverse backgrounds, cultures, and walks of life, Southern University and A&M College is one of 106 historically Black colleges and universities in the United States. It is part of the Southern University System—the nation's only HBCU system—with sister campuses in New Orleans and Shreveport, Louisiana. HBCUs have a proven history of providing excellent education and a solid foundation of academics and culture for its students. For centuries, HBCU alumni have became great successes in all industries, including authors Toni Morrison (Howard University) and Alice Walker (Spellman College); quarterback Jerry Rice (Mississippi Valley State); businessman Herman Cain (Morehouse); film director Spike Lee (Howard University); businesswoman Oprah Winfrey (Tennessee State); activist Marva Collins (Clark Atlanta); and politician Jesse Jackson III (North Carolina A&T) to name a few. The successes of these individuals were influenced by the mentors and high standards they met while attending an HBCU.

It was at the 1879 Louisiana State Constitutional

Convention where Black political leaders P.B.S. Pinchback, T. T. Allain, and Henry Demas, decided to establish an institution "for the education of persons of color". [1] While slavery and segregation, of course, played a large role in the separation of Blacks and whites in public facilities and especially in education, the decision of these three leaders would prove to be historic and critical to the development of Black intellectuals in the state and for generations to come.

In April 1880, exactly one year after the Convention, the Louisiana General Assembly chartered Southern University which had only one building in New Orleans. Later, on March 7, 1881, Southern University opened its doors with twelve students. The University continued to grow but there was not enough land to accommodate its quick expansion and University leaders decided to move the campus to Baton Rouge, under the control of the State Board of Education.

Dr. Joseph Samuel Clark was Southern's first president, overseeing the matriculation of 500 students. He was also the president of the Louisiana Colored Teachers Association. After retiring in 1938, Dr. Clark passed the leadership mantle to his son, Dr. Felton Grandison Clark. Under him, Southern saw even more growth and the student enrollment topped to more than 9,000 students—

---

[1] http://hbcuconnect.com/colleges/82/southern-university-and-a-m-college

an enrollment rate that the Baton Rouge campus has maintained for nearly a century.

Although the growth at Southern spoke volumes about the fight for education equality, there were still opposition. LSU Law School was reluctant to admit any Black American students to their program, so Southern University filed a lawsuit and was allowed to enact their own law program. As a result, the Southern University Law Center was established in 1947. This gave Southern much more notoriety.

During Dr. F.G. Clark's presidency, Southern University established two campuses: one in New Orleans and one in Shreveport. Both the senior and junior Clark set strong foundations as presidents of Southern University which had by now evolved into its own system of campus. (In 2000, the Southern University System established its fifth campus as the SU Agricultural Research and Extension Center, also in Baton Rouge).

The Clarks left the legacy for Southern University and all its campuses to be institutions that would unlock the doors of higher education for generations of young, inquisitive Black Americans. This tradition continues. SU System Presidents Leon G. Netterville , Jesse N. Stone Jr., Joffre T. Whisenton, Delores Spikes, Leon Tarver, Ralph Slaughter, and Ronald Mason Jr., have held the position of president overseeing the development and growth of the five campuses.

In Baton Rouge, Southern University and A&M College remains the system's flagship campus as a comprehensive institution offering four-year, graduate, professional, and doctoral programs. At the time of this book's printing, the Baton Rouge campus offered bachelor's programs in forty-two areas, and nineteen masters, five doctoral, and two associate degree programs. Today, Dr. James L. Llorens is chancellor and Dr. Mason is system president. Like their predecessors, Llorens and Mason hold true to the tradition and esteem of the founding fathers.

> *"While still true to our original mission, Southern University is now a global community with students and faculty representing more than two dozen countries. SU graduates now sit in the boardrooms of Fortune 500 companies, are successful entrepreneurs, educators, and work as scientists and engineers at major laboratories and industries around the world. Remarkably for a small urban campus, 10 of our students have become generals in the United States military."*
>
> ---Dr. James Llorens (2014).

Southern University is ranked as one of the nation's top-tier HBCUs, producing graduates within the top percentages of engineering and nursing fields. Southern has also been recognized as one of the top ten highest producers of bachelor's degrees awarded to Black Americans in the United States. [1]

Many people make the assumption that there is not a diverse student population at historically Black colleges and universities simply because the majority of the students have one race in common. Well, this is simply not the case. At Southern University, specifically, students and faculty come from all over the nation and world and bring a wide spectrum of cultures, ethnicities, and religions.

Additionally, there is an expansive diversity of experiences that these individuals bring from their youth. As I looked at this wide diversity, I realized the significance of an institution like Southern University and why HBCUs are still relevant today. These campuses are a mixing bowl of backgrounds, life experiences, and social economic statuses. Each person is unique in their own way, yet on the campus of Southern University, they are poised to become a *Southern Great*.

The alumni of HBCUs like Southern University represent different beginnings, each beginning fits together like puzzle pieces to create a future of success and excellence that point back to Southern University. Now, I'm not saying that just because these individuals attended Southern University that they were destined for success. No, their success would have more than likely been achieved no matter what university they attended because of their intrinsic motivation to succeed. However, the individual choices that led to their successes helped to leave an indelible mark on the university that educated and poured into their impressionable minds. The accomplishments of these individuals after graduating from Southern University are clear indications that this HBCU took them from their beginnings—be it meager, negative, or average—to a positive, successful future.

I had the pleasure of interviewing each of these Southern Greats over a course of three years while writing this book. Their backgrounds range from small town Louisiana to New York City to Los Angeles to Scotland. Everyone has a different beginning – one that is definitive of his or her personal journey. These Southern Greats lend the story of their beginnings here to demonstrate that success is discovered while on the journey and not handed over at birth.

THE GREATS

I sought to complete one challenge in writing this book. That challenge was to identify and interview Southern University alumni whose lives and careers speak about the character traits that are critical in order to stay on the path of success after graduating from one of the nation's leading historically Black universities and to identify the root evidence of how potential can be harnessed at a collegiate level.

I sat with forty-six alumni who have earned the title of Southern Greats.

Allow me to introduce them and show you how their vast backgrounds, their molding at Southern University, and the challenges of their corporate paths all blend to offer teachable characteristics necessary for you to become successful in any arena.

Let's begin.

HOWARD WHITE

BUILDING CHARACTER

I'm a firm believer that a person's background does not determine their destination nor their future success. Meet **Irving "Jimmie" Matthews**, a successful owner of two Ford dealerships in Central Florida. Today, he is a great distance from his place of birth in New Iberia, Louisiana. However, Mr. Matthews' geographical distance is not what he takes pride in the most. As we sat and visited, he spoke of his parents having the vision to relocate the family of four from agricultural-based New Iberia to Lake Charles, Louisiana, less than 90 miles away. This move helped to change the course of his life and led him to make different choices that would improve his future. In Lake Charles, his life experiences and opportunities were broad in spite of being poor in the segregated South. When you hear Mr. Matthews speak of growing up in a Lake Charles' working class community in the 1960s, you learn about the love of his close-knit family. His first entrepreneurial endeavor was starting a lawn care business that included "backbreaking lawn and gardening work". Like most young men at the time, Mr. Matthews wanted to find a way to earn his own money. What better way than mowing lawns? Being in charge of his own lawn care business brought many responsibilities that taught him the valuable lessons that he would later use as an adult. Mr. Matthews gets excited about the opportunity he had as a 16-year-old businessman, saying this was a stepping stone toward becoming the entrepreneur he is today.

Having to own and operate a business gave him the ability and knowledge to repair and fix almost anything, he said. It was really out of necessity that he had to fix broken mowers and other equipment. This also developed his appreciation for the mechanical side, but more importantly, he says, he learned the "people side" of business and how important it is for businessmen to put people first. "I employ this thought process when running my dealerships. If I take care and treat my employees with respect and care, they will take care of my clients and my car dealerships," said Mr. Matthews.

Many people in business understand the concept of building a community within their place of employment. This type of community builds camaraderie and respect between the boss and employees. Now, this does not mean that the boss has to try to be friends with employees in order to earn their respect. Instead, the boss cultivates a sense of community within the business where the people who work there develop a passion for the job and for the product or services being sold. Their passion begins to match that of the boss and other corporate leaders. This only comes as a result of leaders showing respect to employees and understanding the people side of the business.

Mr. Matthews expanded his business sense while taking courses in business management, accounting, and marketing at Southern University. He learned the value of hard work and the value of people---values that permeate the campus, traditions, and mission of Southern University.

"Southern University was the place I wanted to go to. It was the legacy," said **Pamela Whitley,** who is a third-generation Southern University alumnae.

During the summer enrichment program at Southern, she met instructors who set the foundation for students to come to the university prepared, at all levels, and without labels like remedial, she said.

"Over the course of several years, we had instructors who really were there to make sure you learned the materials. We had professors who really cared about what we were doing," she said. "Even though we had the support of instructors and administration, we also support each other on our journey….At Southern, we built strong networks and once we left (the university), we were all family."

Ms. Whitley, who is an electrical engineer at Federation Aviation Authority, said, "My A-HA moment was realizing that Southern had prepared me and I am as good as everybody else." She remembers being a 22-year-old, Black female engineer overseeing more than twenty white, male senior engineers whose initial reaction was to resist her. She used the lessons from Southern of valuing people in order to earn their professional respect and to have her team respond positively. Once this happened, she said, "I believed then that my engineering degree from Southern University prepared me to do whatever I wanted to do."

Like Ms. Whitley, **Darrell Warner,** vice president for Boeing in their space division, comes from a lineage of Southern Greats including his older brothers and sisters. For years, Warner would ride the winding roads from Bogalusa to Baton Rouge with his siblings. The days and nights that Mr. Warner spent with his older brother Clyde and his friends on campus gave Mr. Warner complete exposure to Southern—and he grew to love it.

"I knew I was coming to Southern University. It had chosen me," he told me as he smiled.

But, that wasn't the case for **Milton Scott.**

"I was not supposed to be at Southern University!" he said.

Like many young men, Mr. Scott grew up playing football and knew that a football scholarship would be his pathway to a college education and to success. However, when the opportunity to quarterback at Tennessee State

University fell through, Mr. Scott was caught off guard and had to think of a backup plan fast. He knew that he would still attend a college or university. The question was where and he did not know. But, he was motivated to make his parents proud, even if it was not at the university of his first choice.

Mr. Scott knew that even though his parents had only a fifth-grade and eighth-grade education, they expected better for him. "I was caught without a plan B. This forced me to go to Southern and work at a plantation in Jackson, Louisiana, to pay for college," said Mr. Scott.

His plan B became his best choice that changed his life for the better.

Mr. Scott's experience demonstrated that although things don't work out like envisioned, the opportunities that arrive on an alternative route can be more beneficial to reaching specific goals. Not every destination requires the same path. Each destination will bring its own unique experiences within that path. We must remember that the goal is to arrive at the destination prepared and with passion. Each route on life's journey is paved with opportunity after opportunity to learn and grow. When one route doesn't turn out the way originally planned, it does not mean that the journey should be forfeit or that it should remain stagnant. Rather, it demands that character and an attitude of determination be developed to know and believe that success will come in one way or another. This renewed character and spirit of determination will make the decision to learn what went wrong, get back on the path, and travel to the next destination. This is critical to overcoming obstacles and roadblocks in any area of life.

After graduating from Southern, Mr. Scott became the first Black partner at the Arthur Anderson Accounting Firm.

What a great accomplishment for an aspiring football player from a small town in Louisiana. Had Mr. Scott chosen not to take an alternative route or not to give His best with plan B, he may have ended up staying in his hometown wondering what could have been. He and associates at the Arthur Anderson Accounting Firm were thankful that he chose to continue on his journey with Southern University as his alternative path.

"Even though I was from a poor background, I had rich life that was greatly enhanced by the stories that my grandfather would share with me when we were fishing. His stories made me want to see and do more. It also helped me realize that my talent and skills could take me around the world if I kept learning and growing," said **Dexter Henderson**

Harvey, Louisiana, is a small town in Jefferson Parish, not widely known by those outside of the state. However, it was the place where Henderson learned to be appreciative of humble beginnings and the support of family and friends. The local community is what Mr.

Henderson appreciates the most about Harvey, saying it was the glue that held him together and helped him to be better than people expected him to be. The support from this small town eventually guided him to make the decision to not give up nor turn down any opportunities for success.

This was what the strength of a group of people—a community—can do for one human being!

It is important to realize that communities often live their dreams and hopes through their youth and young adults. The community prepares their youth as much as they know how and then they launch their protégés out to be more than they are or more than they could become. These communities give the next generation the character traits necessary to gain a better life.

"As an All-American football player at West Jefferson High School in Harvey, LA, it was the words of encouragement throughout the neighborhood that made me realized that I could become something great," Mr. Henderson said.

He experienced a sense of community and encouragement—and found the same characteristics of community throughout the Jaguar Nation, from the bordering neighborhoods in Scotlandville, Louisiana, to the bluffs of the Mississippi at the back of the campus.

Mr. Henderson said he was challenged to push himself and excel in academics and in life. He experienced a community of like-minded individuals who also had the same goals of success as he did and who encouraged him in his goals.

Understanding history and the value that a community can bring to your life is a trait that **Dr. Warren Valdry** proudly demonstrates. Dr. Valdry was born one generation out of slavery. He and his brother, Leon, were able to overcome their sharecropping roots that began in Pointe Coupé Parish. There, Valdry learned lessons from past generations of sharecroppers who worked tirelessly to create a better life for their children, grandchildren, and great grandchildren. Of the many lessons he learned, he said those specific to hard work and perseverance were on the top of the list.

As we sat in the parlor of his 1800 plantation home on False River on New Roads, Louisiana, he said, "My grandfather, who was born in 1824, always believed that a person should control their own destiny. This is something that I have leaned on and worked to teach others throughout my life."

As a youngster from a small country farm, Dr. Valdry created a table that won first place in a statewide competition. That victory drove him to study architecture at Southern University. "It also taught me that I could translate an idea to reality."

At Southern, Dr. Valdry learned the value of having a goal and a vision, working hard at it, and seeing it through to the end. He said the study of architecture is a precise science and art involving the designing and constructing of buildings, structures, objects, and outdoor spaces. The architect goes through a process of thinking of an idea of something to design and build, then actually bringing it to life in its real form.

Dr. James Freemont (deceased) shared with me how he chose to attend Southern University. It began when he visited the campus with his high school English teacher to talk to her daughter.

"I wounded up staying and earned a 3.9 GPA my freshman year." After that, he knew he was in love with Southern University and that he was supposed to be in college. This was when his life changed for the better.

Dr. Freemont did not need a second encounter with Southern in order to make his decision about attending. He knew for sure then.

This assuredness is shared **Gregory Baranco**, owner of Mercedes of Buckhead, near Atlanta. As a young child, Mr. Baranco literally grew up on the campus of Southern. His grandfather worked with Dr. J.S. Clark on the relocation of Southern University from New Orleans to Baton Rouge in 1914; and his father, Dr. Raymond Baranco, helped to build the university infirmary. Even with his ties and history with the university, the younger Baranco decided to enroll in Tulane University. However, he said, he never forgot about Southern and later, he returned to the place he had already called home so long before.

"I was tired of being in an environment where people were telling me that I couldn't," said Mr. Baranco. "Southern University told me that I could." He said Southern University embraced him and allowed him to flourish in a nurturing academic environment. Southern University cultivated his confidence and helped him become a highly successful car dealer. This is one of the great attributes of Southern University, it supports the possibilities and dreams of the students at time in their lives that they are striving to build their own wings.

As with Mr. Baranco, the campus of Southern University was a second home for the **Rev. Byron Stevenson** who attended Southern University Laboratory School and took pride in the university from the first day he walked onto the campus. "As a freshman at Southern, I knew that I was now a bona-fide student. Even though I had spent my whole life on campus from kindergarten to twelfth grade, I was now a legitimate Southern University student. And it just felt good," he said.

Greg Foster, the son of a Gramblinite, said it was the feeling of Southern that made him cross over to attend and graduate from Southern—Grambling's rival HBCU.

"I can remember going to Grambling for a football game and Southern took over. That atmosphere was magical and second to none. I knew [from then] that I was going to Southern," said Mr. Foster.

Childhood and adolescent experiences oftentimes leave an indelible mark on our heart and mind with very vivid positive and negative memories. These experiences can propel someone to achieve the kind of successes that they couldn't imagine achieving otherwise. It takes them on a journey to places never before seen in order to teach them the value of perseverance.

Clarence "CJ" Bland's journey to and through Southern University led him to become an electrical engineer. "Growing up in inner city New Orleans, I saw the good and the bad of life, and it made me realize what I wanted to pursue. This led me to attend Dillard to obtain a physics degree and then graduate from Southern University [with a degree] in electrical engineering," said Mr. Bland.

He overcame the severe illness of his mother during his last years at Dillard, chose to confront this negative experience, conquer it, and then find strength from it to continue his education. Electrical engineering was where he found his passion and where he could express his creativity and innovative mind as well.

Mr. Bland spoke of a brief experience he had with a professor that taught him a lifelong lesson about hardwork and value. "I remember once that I had an 89.9 average and was lobbying for an A, but the professor said to me, 'You earned a B, and in life, people will give you what you earn. Don't be expected to receive things that you don't earn.'"

From that point on, Mr. Bland never lobbied for success, but worked diligently for it and saw the value in that hard work. At Southern, his professors taught him the skills necessary to be an excellent electrical engineer who would work meticulously and relentlessly.

For Southern University alum **Elliot Jerome Lyons,** great success was not achieved without painstaking effort. "I can remember spending days in cotton fields, chopping cotton with other people at the age of 13 or 14. This built my foundation for hardwork," said the corporate executive. Living through a life of hard labor just so that your family could survive and have an opportunity at a better life must have been stressful and difficult for Mr. Lyons. However, he had a vision for his life and a goal to take what life handed him and make it a success.

He graduated in the top ten percent of his high school class in Wynn, Arkansas, and had one scholarship offer which was from Southern University. This, in and of itself, was a great accomplishment. He said he took pride in it, knowing he would attend one of the greatest historically Black universities. Nationally, Southern University had already established the tradition and reputation of being an institution where young and intellectual Black Americans could challenge their minds, exercise their creativity, maximize their individuality, and accomplish great things in any academic field. Mr. Lyons knew that studying at Southern University was his opportunity to achieve greatness for himself and for his family. His hard work in the cotton fields and in high school led him to a university that would propel him to even greater success. For this opportunity, he was extremely proud. He and twin brother **Vincent Scott Lyons** moved to Southern University.

"I remember as a top five graduate, knowing that I was smarter and better prepared than my high school classmates, but I was overlooked for college scholarships and under-promoted by my high school because I am Black. Southern [University] gave my brother and me a $625 engineering scholarship. This made the difference in starting our journey to be engineers," said Mr. Vincent Scott Lyons.

"All things happen for a reason at the time it happens. You may not understand the reason or benefit at the time. But, if you are looking for an excuse to not do something, there are plenty of excuses to stop you," Mr. Elliot Lyons said.

This sentiment holds true for attorney **Thomas "TNT" Todd** who refused to see childhood difficulties as hindrances to his future. In fact, he viewed his meager beginning as a springboard.

"I grew up in a one-room house," said Mr. Todd, "to [becoming] SGA President of my high school, to catching the L&N Train to go to Southern. With this springboard, I was able to go on and be a nationally known attorney."

> **The ability to see life's difficulties as springboards is what separates the go-getters from the excuse-makers.**

This chapter defined the word "beginning" and presented how these Southern Greats' beginnings set their futures in motion. Everything, including the world, began with its Creator, and its beginning sets the precedence for its future. Do you remember your beginning? Do you remember when success was created or just starting to be achieved in your life? How did it shape or determine your future? Every story has a beginning; every leader has a story. It doesn't matter what your starting point or beginning is. What you should always remember is that you have a choice to decide where your end will be.

For these Southern Greats, their humble—and for some meager—beginnings marked the start of a journey that led to Southern University and on to success.

REFLECTIONS FROM THE BLUFF:

List two great challenges that you have faced in your life.

_____
_____
_____
_____
_____
_____

What are some of the lessons that you learned from these experiences?

_____
_____
_____
_____
_____
_____

What will you do differently the next time you face a seemingly insurmountable challenge?

_____
_____
_____
_____
_____

HOWARD WHITE

IT'S ALL ABOUT THE LOVE

Great experiences can lend themselves to a great learning and memorable environment. These experiences help to create new and different perspectives and, in turn, aid in learning new things. Moreover, when someone is open to learn new things and have a great experience, they also develop an open mind for change.

The first experience is something that everyone has in common, and it is something we all remember. The first experience I'm referring to is that first time you experience Southern University. We, Southern University graduates, refer to Southern as Lady Southern, that beautiful jewel that sits on the bluffs of the Mississippi River. No matter who has the pleasure of attending Southern University, they all say that Lady Southern has touched their lives.

I would be remiss if I didn't speak about the first time that I experienced Southern University and came face-to-face with its campus. I previously mentioned that while I was a junior in high school, I had a chance to attend a six-week, on-campus program in engineering known as the Engineering Summer Institute, ESI, at Southern University. Now, as a country boy from the small town of Prentiss, Mississippi, this was one heck of an experience to be able to come to the big city and attend what was one of the largest HBCUs in the country at the time. It was intimidating to be a part of something so much bigger than I could imagine. Truthfully, I was more excited about the ladies I'd be able to meet and that I would be away from home for an extended period time for the first time. Who wouldn't be excited as sixteen year old boy?

Little did I know that those six weeks when I participated in the ESI program would forever change my life. No one ever realizes that the small encounters and experiences throughout the course of their lives will eventually lead them directly to what they will do and who they will become in the future. After the program was all said and done, it was not the beautiful ladies or the big city that left a lasting mark on my life. Rather, it was the great friendships and experiences that I had with fellow ESI students and with the professors who took the time out to teach us, high school juniors, what engineers do and what we could expect from college that had the most significant affect on me. I had some great times and learned great lessons from our counselors: Stan, Ruby, Karen, David, and others. They took their responsibility seriously and had high expectations for us at the close of the program. Yet, they still allowed us to be kids and have fun.

When I speak to various Southern Greats, they all get excited when they speak of the first time they fell in love with Southern University. This is what we Southern University alumni all have in common—no matter our backgrounds or our beginnings—we are all joined by our love for Southern University. No matter what year it was when we first attended Southern, the love for the University is still the same. This affection we all have for our alma mater is because we all benefited from the great lessons at Southern University.

Great experiences and a memorable environment create great learning opportunities.

Any Southern Great you speak with has fond memories of being at the university, and the late Dr. James Freemont is no exception. The Atlanta-based OB-GYN had a bright glow in his eyes when he spoke about his first time stepping on the campus of Southern University. Dr. Freemont is originally from Monroe, Louisiana, and graduated from Carroll High School in 1960. In high school, he was an above average student who was excited just to complete high school. For him and his family, this was quite an accomplishment. As a result, he hadn't put much thought into where he would attend college, and he certainly hadn't put much thought into attending Southern University.

As fate would have it, one day one of his teachers asked him to drive her to the city of Baton Rouge. At that time, he didn't know that this was the city where Southern University was located. After he arrived there and spent time on Southern's campus, he did not want to go back home to Monroe. He enrolled in Southern on the spot. Thanks to Dr. G. Leon Netterville, the Southern University president at that time, D. Freemont did not have to go back to Monroe. He started classes and later finished his first semester with a 3.9 grade point average, and didn't look back. He had definitely fallen in love with Lady Southern.

The journey that we all take in our lives doesn't always lead us to where we want to be or to where we envision we need to me. For Dr. Freemont, he never envisioned a future for himself beyond high school. However, a spur of the moment car ride took him on a different journey that changed his perspective and changed his life for the better.

You may remember me writing in the earlier chapter about Southern graduates and twins, Vincent and Elliott Lyons from Wynn, Arkansas. When I asked them about their campus experiences and fondest memories of Southern University, they both talked about those early days on campus and the friendships they forged in Jones Hall, the freshman dorm. Everyone remembers college as being a time of intense study sessions, difficult professors, and even more difficult coursework. However, hanging out in dorm rooms, cultivating lasting friendships, and creating memories are some of the best experiences of being in college. Living in these close quarters, sharing a room and bathroom, making meals together, and just hanging out are moments that are remembered the most.

There are many other Southern University graduates who have fond memories of their first experience on Southern's campus. People like **Mr. Joseph Stewart**, who shared with me that his time at Southern was a fun and joyous time in his life. He spoke of many great things about Southern University like, "[having] many professors believe in you until you would believe in yourself."

Mr. Stewart is a former Vice President at Kellogg, who has visited with all of the White House administrations since President Gerald Ford. He is a man who considers the late Nelson Mandela and Bishop Desmond Tutu as associates and friends. Yet, Mr. Stewart counts his time at Southern University and his professors as the most integral time in life with some of the most important set of people he has met. At Southern, he received a "personalized education that would turn your motivation into success."

Retired U.S Lieutenant General Russel Honore' holds the same thoughts about his first experience at Southern as Mr. Stewart. The morning I interviewed General Honore', he was preparing to travel to Cuba, but still made the time to tell me about his love for Southern University. "Southern University met me where I was and pulled me up the hill. It was a caring system that made time for me and gave me a couple of 'Do Overs'," he said.

His first experience was similar to coming home and being embraced by family, he said. He holds fond memories of the stability, support, and encouragement he received from the professors and staff. To him, "Southern valued the importance of investing in students," he said.

The investment Southern University pours in its students helps to produce many great professionals like **Darrell Warner,** currently the vice president for Boeing in their space division. Mr. Warner comes from a long line of Southernites and his Southern University lineage is well-known by many.

Mr. Warner had the advantage of having older brothers and sisters who attended Southern University. His first experience at Southern University was travelling from Bogalusa, to move his sister into her dorm. Later, he would ride back and forth with her in the evening as she attended graduate school. He grew to have a strong knowledge of Southern University's campus, and in turn, he grew to love it. "I knew I was coming to Southern University. It had chosen me," he told me as he smiled.

The same was the case for Mr. Todd who I briefly mentioned in the previous chapter. From the moment he took his first train ride to Baton Rouge, he felt as if he was entering a foreign land. He said, "As I came on the campus of Southern University, I thought it was one of the most beautiful places that I had ever seen; *it actually was*. The moss, the big trees, and the Mississippi River made me realize that I was at home." And he would be "at home" at Southern University for the next seven years, earning both his bachelor's and law degrees.

At the 1969 SU vs. Grambling football game, **Dennis Brown** fell in love with Southern University just as Mr. Todd had. Dennis said, "When Southern's band came into Grambling's stadium, it was something about the sound that made Southern feel different. Even though Southern was the visiting team, they we were at home."

Not only did the music of Southern University's band have a lasting impact on Mr. Brown, but the love and support from people in the community whose lives had been touched or changed by Southern also had an impact on him. The fall of 1972 was the height of civil unrest on Black campuses across America. Two students, Denver Smith and Leonard Brown, were killed by white sheriff deputies while participating in a peaceful student protest.

These two victims were unarmed students gathering at a building on Southern University's campus protesting the administration officials and their policies. Students wanted to voice their grievances about not having a greater voice in school affairs and about the resignations of certain administrators.

On November 16, 1972, several students stormed the administration building in an attempt to seek the release of students who had been arrested for protesting the night before. It was reported that state police and sheriff's deputies entered the administration building with firearms and tear gas in order to thwart the attempts of these students. What occurred later was an utter tragedy. Denver Smith and Lenard Brown were found dead after the state police and deputies stormed the building.

Dennis Brown remembers this time very well. "When Smith and Brown were murdered on campus, the campus was shut down," he said. "Most of the students did not have anywhere to go. The community of Baton Rouge opened their arms to provide us, the students, with a place to stay. This demonstrated the love that the community had – and still has – for Southern University."

Southern University has always been surrounded by a city that thrives on its sense of community. Those within and outside of the campus take a sense of ownership and love for Southern University students, always being there to help in any way they can.

As I sat and listen to Mr. Brown share this story, I realize how important the whole community is in helping to shape and mold us as individuals. When you look at the connection that Baton Rouge has shared with Southern and the students, it is evident that the Baton Rouge community has been an "X" factor in the lives of every student that has attended Southern.

This is how we should strive to live our lives and really become an "X" factor in our community on a daily basis. Just imagine that. If we all got back to being an "X" factor how great this world would be.

Bernice Washington, who's from the small town of Goat Hill in north Louisiana, moved from this community of only about 80 people to the large community of thousands of Southern University students. She experienced the same love and acceptance at Southern that she was so used to from home. She even met her sweetheart and husband, Lt. Colonel Lyman Washington at Southern. "I was watching the ROTC march on campus and saw the leader. I always said I came to Southern for two things: a husband and a degree. So why not choose the leader of one the largest organizations on campus? Long story short, I asked Lyman his name and introduced myself. The next time that I saw him he did not remember my name, but I didn't give up. The rumor was that I was stalking him. He finally wore down and the rest is history."

Jeniffer Harper-Taylor, President of the Siemens Foundation, enrolled in Southern University sight unseen. "The summer after my graduation my dad brought me down to Baton Rouge. I remember that he talked about Tony's Seafood and crawfish."

She said she met a lifelong friend in her roommate. "She was a person that brought me from a selfish person to a someone that would learn to share and care about others. Being in a suite with eight other women and sharing (one) bathroom you had to learn to share and get along. We all became a posse'."

It's not just academics and a sense of community, but also love that is gained from being at Southern University. Another Southern Great, Dr. Darrel Carmen had to think for a moment or two about his first love of Southern University. He grew up in a family with more than eight other Southern University graduates so he was reared on and around Southern. After a few moments, he said, "I knew that I was in love with Southern University when during my first homecoming all of the alumni came back to share with us students. This helped me realize the value of the education that I was receiving."

Hall of Fame baseball player **Lou Brock** also knows about finding your love at Southern University. He had traveled to Higher Ground Outreach Church in Baton Rouge with a message on diabetes the day we spoke. On that day, he shared with me about how he first started playing baseball in college. "I had lost my academic scholarship because of having less than the required 3.0 GPA and was hanging out at baseball practice shagging fly balls with a high school student while trying to figure out what I would do. See, I couldn't go back home because my hometown thought that I was smart and would make it very easily. Then, for some reason I fainted and when I came to the coach ask me if I played baseball? I told him that I did in high school. So he gave me five swings on the bat. A couple went over the fence and the rest were hits. So the coach offered me a scholarship and I was able to stay at Southern." Mr. Brock would later star for Southern University's baseball team and have a Hall of Fame career with the St. Louis Cardinals. Today, Mr. Brock is an ordained minister, traveling and speaking to audiences with a message about Christ and about diabetes.

National freelance sportscaster **James Verrett**, who has worked with Fox, ESPN and various other networks, remembers the first time he fell in love with Southern University. Without hesitation, he said he knew he loved Southern during an Alvin Ailey American Dance Theater performance in the F.G. Clark Activity Center. "I was used to seeing athletes perform, but Southern gave me a chance to see athletes perform with such grace, style, and rhythm. This most likely would not have been possible to see if Southern was not a Black college and was not here in Baton Rouge." Seeing the dance performance gave Mr. Verrett a new definition of an athlete, exposure to the arts, and an appreciation for dance.

The great experiences at Southern University lead to a great learning and memorable environment for its students. All of the Southern Greats featured in this chapter, and many others, have been able to receive the valuable gifts of love, pride in what Southern University represents, and the sense of community Southern University has to offer to its students. This gives evidence to the importance of our historically Black colleges and universities and what they impart to our communities, our culture, and our history.

More importantly, this stresses the importance of being surrounded by a loving and supportive environment in your formative years. It's critical to be in an environment that challenges you see your own possibilities, that allows you to make mistakes, and demands that you to learn and grow from those mistakes. This is what Southern University has done and continues to do for so many.

REFLECTIONS FROM THE BLUFF:

1.   Spend a few minutes and think of the supportive environments that you have been in over your lifetime:_____

_____
_____
_____
_____
_____
_____
_____
_____

2.   Take time to write down some of mistakes that you made and the lessons that you learned while you were in these environment:_____

_____
_____
_____
_____
_____
_____
_____
_____

HOWARD WHITE

REFINED BY MENTORS

The many successful individuals who attended historically Black colleges and universities attribute the bulk of their success to the role models and mentors who guided them through matriculation. These mentors are professors, coaches, band directors, and academic advisors who challenged and encouraged them to relentlessly pursue every one of their dreams and to be excellent throughout that pursuit.

Mentors... They help to make Me who I am and will be Each of the forty-six Southern University Greats I interviewed attribute the bulk of their success to the role models and mentors they found while attending college. These professors, coaches, band members/directors, and academic advisors where consistent mentors who challenged and encouraged them in their academic and personal pursuits.

The word mentor is defined as a wise and trusted counselor or teacher, an influential senior sponsor, or supporter. When I read this definition of the word mentor I cannot help but smile and think about all of the mentors who have poured into my life and who continue to pour into me.

The role of a mentor is a critical one. They are not only leaders, but they also play the role of a confidant, a brother/sister, a teacher, and a friend. Mentors encourage and challenge their mentees to be more than they (the mentee) could ever see themselves being.

When I think about Southern University, I think about the many professors, deans, and counselors who chose to work at Southern University because they wanted to impact and mold the minds of young, intellectual, Black boys and girls. Most of us were young and naive when we entered Southern, and this naiveté prevented us from seeing pass ourselves and pass the thrill of being away from home at college on our own. Many of Southern's professors, deans, and counselors were individuals that could have been working and teaching at almost any institution in the world. However, they chose to teach us; they chose to be our mentors. And, boy, did we need it.

As impressionable young college students at Southern University, we thought that we knew it all and didn't need much advice. Little did we know, we would need the advice and counsel of our mentors to get us through. I believe that everyone should have a mentor in their lives to help them get through every new phase.

When I think of a mentor, I think of the late Dr. Wesley Cornelius McClure Sr. When I first met Dr. McClure at Southern University, he was the Vice Chancellor of Academic Affairs and was responsible for all things that involved student registration. Dr. McClure was a man who at times had an unapproachable demeanor that you noticed from afar. He always looked as if he was serious, about business, and on a mission. All of the students were intimidated by him, including me. His stance and stare, as he stood with his arms folded, would often say, "Don't bother or dare interrupt me." But, the same demeanor that intimidated some students also made other students respect Dr. McClure. It made you want to know more about him.

My first personal interaction with Dr. McClure was as a student worker for registration. Ironically, I was referred to him by one of my future fraternity brothers, Anthony Pegues. Anthony had warned me to never be late when meeting with Dr. McClure. If so, it might be better that you just don't show up at all, Anthony said. The morning that I was scheduled to meet him, we had to be in the F.G. Clark Activity Center for 7 a.m. I made sure that I followed Anthony's advice. I arrived around 6:30 a.m. and picked up my radio and assignment. Around 6:45 Dr. McClure showed up and began to go down his list of names. One by one he would call names and if you were not there at 6:50 am, he simply said, "That person no longer exists to me and when they do show up tell them there is no need to stay. Tell them they can just go back to bed."

It may sound mean and shocking, and that's because it was. However, it was what we all needed; we needed someone like him who was not afraid to be stern and not take excuses. We also needed someone who was going to teach us how valuable an individual's time is and how valuable our time and word are.

And what was the lesson learned? The lesson learned was to always be on time. No, not to Dr. McClure. He would often say, to be 'on time' is to be early; to show up at the designated time is to be late; and to come later than the meeting time, well, there is no need to come at all.

To a young college student being mentored by Dr. McClure, this lesson did not seem very important right away, but over time, however, it is one of the best lessons anyone can learn.

This is a lesson that I try to subscribe to even to this day. I have found that by taking Dr. McClure's advice and showing up early, good things can happen and they often do. There is a saying that "there is always a meeting before the meeting" and the only way you can participate in that meeting is to show up early.

MENTORS DEMAND MORE

While sitting on the back balcony at his home in Austin, I asked Dexter Henderson, Vice President with IBM, to talk about some of his Southern University mentors. Immediately, he smiled as he spoke about his mentor Dr. Earl Marcelle.

Mr. Henderson had come to Southern as an All-American football player out of New Orleans' West Jefferson High. He came from an impressive past. However, Dr. Marcelle was not impressed with Mr. Henderson's All-American background the way other people he had been. Let's just say that Dr. Marcelle did not care about how well Mr. Henderson could catch and run a football. Instead, Dr. Marcelle wanted to grow and challenge Mr. Henderson's mind. He believed that Mr. Henderson could be more than what he was and more than who everyone saw him as.

Since Mr. Henderson was a football player, he would occasionally miss tests because of away football games. Even though these tests were all excused and he could make them up, Dr. Marcelle would not let him make up these tests. Instead of taking a makeup test, Dr. Marcelle would require Mr. Henderson to do a research paper of at least fifty pages on a new and innovative technology; then present his paper to the class. Of course, writing a research paper was certainly not a welcoming alternative to taking a test. And at the time, Mr. Henderson thought that this was cruel and unusual punishment.

As he thought back to the experience, he said, "It was professors like Dr. Marcelle that challenged me to think and look beyond the regular. It was this experience of having to research new technologies that prepared me for my transition to Corporate America. It was having to present a paper to Dr. Marcelle and the class that helped me to be comfortable with speaking in front groups." Mr. Henderson also said, this helped to develop his presentation skills and become more comfortable before crowds. "What I thought was punishment, it was actually preparing me for my career with IBM," he said.

Lt. General Honore' told of a similar experience he had with his mentor Major White. As he recalled it, Major White had given him an assignment to teach a class in map reading. General Honore' admitted to me that he did not put the time in and failed miserably. Major White asked General Honore' what happened and the then-cadet Honore' told him "I don't like to teach and don't plan on being a teacher." Major White told him that if he would be an officer in the US Army he would be teaching on a daily basis. Major White then told General Honore' that he would have to do the lesson over. General Honore' said that he learn two great lessons from this interaction: first, he must be fully prepared the first time regardless of the task, and second, he must be willing to give people "Do Overs" or a second chance to live up to their true potential. Major

White had given him a "Do Over" and the opportunity to live up to his true potential.

Mr. Henderson was equally excited as he talked about his chairman of Southern's computer science, Dr. Leroy Roquemore, another mentor. He spoke of how the this mentor would take time to talk and provide him with career guidance. It was Dr. Roquemore who made sure that he interviewed with IBM, the only company where Mr. Henderson has worked since graduating from Southern University.

A common thread among these Southern Greats are their varied mentors who challenged them to be more that they thought they could be. Corporate executive Mr. Elliot Lyons was one of them.

When I asked Elliot Lyons about some of the people who served as mentors to him, he first shared some words of wisdom about mentoring. He said to be a mentor, you must be unselfish and have your mentee's best interest at heart. He spoke of two mentors at Southern University who changed his life for the better. One was Dean M.Q. Burrell and the other was Dr. Delores Spikes.

"Dean Burrell would often go out of his way to discuss our future beyond Southern. In these conversations he would go out of his way to make sure that we understood we can always be what we wanted to be no matter where we had started. He always challenged you as a person," Mr. Lyons said. "He personally helped us financially by finding scholarship dollars that made it easy for my brother and I to focus on school."

At the end of their first year at Southern University, Mr. Lyons and his twin brother Vincent didn't know how they were going to pay for school and expenses the following year because of their family's financial situation. Dr. Delores Spikes, who was then the Vice Chancellor of Academic Affairs, took time out of her day to sit and talk with the Lyons twins about their situation.

She showed them empathy and compassion. She even took the time to learn about them as individuals. Out of that meeting Dr. Spikes found the resources to help ensure that finances would not keep the Lyons twins from earning mechanical engineering degrees from Southern University. Ironically, by the time they graduated Suma Cum Laude, Dr. Spikes became the first, and only to-date, female president of the Southern University System and personally handed them their degrees during the commencement ceremony. They left Southern not only confident in their abilities as engineers, but also confident that they had chosen the perfect university, one that met their academics and personal needs. For the Lyons twins, Southern was not just a school; it was their home away from home, where the administration cared about every facet of the students' lives.

Each and every Southern Great interviewed had several professors, deans, or counselors who were true mentors to them. These individuals often opened the doors to their homes and their families. They also spent numerous hours outside of the classroom with their mentees making sure they understood the academic lessons as well as the life lessons of responsibility and leadership being taught to them.

Dr. James Bryant was one of these dedicated mentors. Mrs. Bernice Washington remembers well the lessons of leadership and responsibility Dr. Bryant taught her. "There was one semester where I was working on a project and it ran into the Christmas holiday. It was actually Christmas Eve when I finished the project and got a grade of C."

"I began to cry because of this grade, and I asked Dr. James Bryant how could I have gotten a C." He said to me, "Excellence is excellence and you are judged by your results not by the effort you give."

"These words taught me that I had to produce results and I would be measured by my outcome and not my output," she said.

Moreover, Dr. Bryant's words of wisdom propelled Mrs. Bernice Washington to graduate fourth in her class and go on to have a stellar career at Bayer as one of their top executives in the hospital division.

It says a great deal about you when out of all of the professors at one school, a student remembers you for what you taught them in the classroom, and those same lessons follow them to their professions and through their lives. Now, even the next generation is reaping the benefits of what these mentors have sown into the lives of Southern Greats.

It is truly a commendable accomplishment when someone speaks of your role in their lives as being "monumental". I had the privilege of hearing that from another Southern Great, Mrs. Jeniffer Harper-Taylor, who used this very word to describe the level of impact she received from her mentor Dr. Emma Hines, the Dean of the College of Arts and Humanities. "Dr. Hines was the hardest professor that I experienced. She stressed mastering your voice and phonetics. She truly turned me from a Southern Bell to what she termed a 'World Woman'," Mrs. Harper-Taylor said.

From lessons in leadership and responsibility to lessons in voice and phonetics, there's quite a great deal of things a mentor can teach a mentee that are important and will inevitably lead to their success.

Dr. Leonard Haynes, an executive with the federal government, is another one of those mentors who words of wisdom and life lessons changed many lives. James Verrett, the freelance sportscaster you read about in the previous chapter, said, "Dr. Haynes introduced me to philosophy and caused me to think differently, [to] look at all of the issues." Bishop Joseph Walker also said, "Dr. Haynes would challenge you to go beyond you and not only look within, but also look outside for the answer and the solution. "

If you had the fortune to meet Dr. Haynes you would agree with them both. I had the privilege of speaking with Dr. Haynes who told me:

> **Mentors prepare you, point you, and then push you.**

For Mr. Verrett, Dr. Haynes and Dr. Robert "Bob" Rene' were the prepare-point-push mentors." Dr. Rene, a news reporter in the early '80s who motivated me to pursue a job as a reporter. Growing up you did not see many African-American men in front of the camera on TV," said Verrett. "Dr. Rene's teaching and sharing with me about being the best that you could be is something that I still pull from today. We still maintain a true friendship to this day."

When I asked Mr. Joseph Stewart, former Vice President of Kellogg, about the importance of having a mentor, he said that it all started with his brother-in-law, Mr. David Hall, who had been commissioned in ROTC and majored in food and nutrition. "Food and nutrition was not necessarily a popular major for a man in the 1960s, however because of David, I had someone who I could mirror and model. This is what got me to start working in food service and ultimately led to my first job as Assistant Director of Dining at Jackson State University." This start is what eventually led to Mr. Stewart becoming Director of Food and Nutrition for the Washington DC Public School System and later a Senior Vice President of Kellogg.

Mentors have the ability to motivate individuals to success in their education and their careers. This is exactly what happened for Dennis Brown. Mr. Brown, a former Southern University's National Alumni Federation president, now enjoys life as a motivator and trainer. He is known as Mr. Attitude. When I asked him about who influenced his life, he spoke of his mentors at Southern University that prepared, pointed and pushed him toward success. He first talked about Ms. Lula Thomas. "I remember she told me that I was going to do real good in business. This gave me so much confidence and an attitude to continue forward."

"The professors and deans cared about you as a person and they were also willing to go beyond and take the extra steps to make sure that you succeeded." Mr. Brown said. Then began to talk about Dean of the College of Business, Dr. Brenda Birkett. He said, "Dr. Birkett made every student feel special and would do whatever she could do to make sure that every student succeeded in the classroom and in their chosen careers."

It's one thing for a mentor to make such an impact on their mentee's life that they remember their lessons and words of wisdom years later. But it speaks volumes when a mentor can remain an integral part of their mentee's lives.

Dr. Darrell Carmen has this kind of relationship with his mentor the late Dr. James Freemont. "As a young doctor, I was always calling Dr. Freemont for personal and professional advice. Because of the Southern connection he was always there to listen and provide advice. This type of relationship is priceless," said Dr. Carmen.

Up until his death in July of 2013, Dr. James Freemont was a Southern University alum who consistently served as a mentor for Dr. Carmen. He proudly said that it was his mentors at Southern University who helped to make him who he is today. "I have family members older than me who were doctors. I also had other great Southern graduates who are doctors who helped me and continuously give me advice about my medical career," he said.

Mr. Greg Foster was also encouraged to pursue his career goals and become a better and tougher person by Dr. Birkett. He remembers her telling him, "I am not going to let you waste your gift!" He learned a great deal from Dr. Birkett and other mentors like her who took the time to teach them lessons outside of the college classroom. "...They knew we were ready for anything the world outside Southern could bring," said Mr. Foster of the confidence that mentors had in him and other students.

I had the pleasure of spending some time with Mr. Milton Scott, who was the first African American in the country to make full partner at Arthur Anderson accounting firm. He shared with me how his mentor, U.S. Senator J. Bennett Johnston, made all the difference in helping him choose between being in an accounting firm or becoming a lawyer.

Mr. Scott graduated from Southern University in three years and was accepted to LSU Law School. His original plans were influenced by Senator Johnston who convinced him that he should consider taking a deferment on law school and test out an accounting firm. This wasn't the first time that Senator Johnson had deterred Mr. Scott from law. When asked about the major role that the Senator played in his life and in him determining a career, Mr. Scott said, "Mentors are those people who truly have our best interest [at heart] and they have a unique way of seeing things and implementing them. " Mr. Scott recognized that the Senator's intentions were not to confuse him, but instead to help steer him in a direction that would cause him to not have any regrets about his decisions. After considering the Senator's suggestion, Mr. Scott began a successful accounting career and never looked back. His success is credited to the guidance of one caring mentor.

Mr. Arthur George remembers three individuals who taught him life lessons that changed him for the better. The first person was Dr. Williams who taught him the value of perseverance. He said, "Dr. Williams refused to sign my drop slip and he wanted me to think about why he would not sign it. This made me realize that I could not quit when things got tough. "

Mr. George's second mentor was Dr. James Cross, the Department Chair of Electrical Engineering. His relationship with Dr. Cross showed him that he was not in it alone. Instead, he had mentors that were rooting for his success. "Dr. Cross often stated that, 'I teach it and I care if you get it." Mr. George said. This is a phrase that describes many Southern University professors who relentlessly showed students their own value and the value in what they were teaching.

These mentors knew that those same students would one day be successful professionals because of what they were taught at Southern.

Changing Life's Course

Southern University is and will continue to be full of mentors. I will close this chapter with a story that truly demonstrates the spirit of Southern University. I can fondly remember a couple of situations recently that stressed the power of mentors. The first one was when I was at a Southern University basketball game in 2003. I was in one of those valleys that we all go through in our life. It was a time in my life where I felt defeated and doubted my ability to be successful at anything. I was discouraged, and I needed someone to speak directly to me and to what I was facing.

As I sat there at the game, Mr. T.J. Hurst, a great Southern University supporter and businessman, sat beside me and we talked. I shared with him some of the challenges that I was facing. Then, he began to share with me the importance of focusing on where I wanted to go – my end goal. He challenged me to consider my destination in order to understand my journey. Those are words that I continue to hold on to this day. This interaction made me reflect on the importance of mentors throughout our lives and how if we are open they appear when we need them the most.

My second experience with a Southern mentor was in the spring of 2012. I was talking with Dr. Huey Lawson as he shared with me about his engineering class and how ill-prepared a lot of the incoming students were.

On this Saturday morning at a job fair hosted by our church, Living Faith Christian Center, Dr. Lawson told me how he let his students know that in order to successfully complete his class they would have to meet the required criteria and at that present time the majority of them were long ways away from the required criteria. He didn't attempt to scare them with the thought that they were ill-prepared and would never measure up. Instead, he encouraged these students, pushed them to work hard, and reminded them that it was not an unachievable goal. He promised them that he was going to work harder on their success than they were willing to work. In fact, he added additional class hours on Thursday nights--in addition to the three-hour class on Tuesday nights-- in order to help the students excel. Tough teacher? Yes! Dedicated teacher? Definitely! Many students may not realize that they have a mentor that is openly pouring into their lives and preparing them to excel.

I remember this the most about Southern University's professors – they were always determined to propel their students into the world well prepared and educated. Southern University is an institution that meets you where you are, challenges you, nurtures you, and equips you to be successful in life and career. This is what continues to draw more and more students to Southern University's campus.

We're all familiar with the African Proverb, "It takes a village to raise a child." Mentors hold integral roles within the village which helps a child propel and excel. It takes the great warrior to teach the village to run fast and fight furiously; it takes the wise man to teach how to seek wisdom through all experiences; it takes the great mother to teach the miracle of caring and protection.

I firmly believe that I am who I am because of the influence of others in my life. These mentors inspired and challenged me, and subsequently changed the course of my life.

REFLECTIONS FROM THE BLUFF

Take a few moments to think of the mentors who have help you. List their names. After you have listed their names send them a personal thank you note.

1._____

2._____

3._____

4._____

5._____

Who are the mentors currently in your life?

1._____

2._____

3._____

List the names of potential future mentors and how they will help you achieve your goals.

1._____

_____

2._____

_____

_____

3._____

_____

_____

Following Your True Passion

When we are passionate about things, we give our lives completely to and for it. It consumes our thoughts and our imagination. It is something that brings joy and motivation to push beyond capabilities. When we are zealous, we make decisions solely on how our passion will be impacted—and we labor over the work that is required to succeed. Truly passionate people are not focused exclusively on the immediate occurrences of their lives. In fact, they envision their goal months—even years—away and they begin to plot a deliberate course, follow it, and arrive at a place of accomplishment and success.

Let's discuss this a little more. The word "passion" is defined as any powerful or compelling emotion or feeling.

I have to agree with fellow HBCU Great Oprah Winfrey (Tennessee State University, '75) who said, "**Passion** is energy! Feel the power that comes from focusing on what excites you."

As leadership coach John Maxwell said, the courage to fulfill your vision—your purpose—will come from passion. When you stop and begin to truly focus on what excites you, the energy of it pulls you to accomplish it. Your passion grows, and you are recharged with energy and vitality. It's passion that causes you to continuously pedal on the bicycle of life—with purpose in mind. Passion will drive you to pedal harder and more furiously as you go up mountainous challenges and through the risky forests of opportunities in your journey towards success.

Your passion will fuel your purpose on your journey to success.

So, what *is* your purpose?

That's truly not a rhetorical question. As sure as you are reading this book, you still have the opportunity to fulfill your purpose and chase your passion.

Take a moment and look away from these pages and answer that question. What is your purpose?

The next question you must then ask yourself is, "am I willing to pursue it passionately?"

This is an important question to ask because it will be your fuel to help you continue on your journey. Essentially, you need to develop a total understanding of why you are doing what you are doing. Determining your purpose requires that you think through what you are passionate about and why you are passionate about it. Then decide, what is it that you are to do with the passion and purpose.

Southern Great **Lavell Crump**, known in the entertainment industry as David Banner, told reporters that he'd gotten to a place of depression and it was through meditation that he was able to regroup and revive himself. For this entertainment entrepreneur, music, sound, and voice were his passions. He told the reporters that during his time of mediation, he realized sound was everywhere. Even in the sound of a remote control or a text message, there is sound. And where there was sound, there was a producer. Where there was a producer, there was opportunity for him. That realization brought his purpose into a new realm of opportunity to follow his passion. He began producing commercials, in addition to producing two short films, writing for *Black Enterprise* magazine, and staring on "The Butler", and numerous other movies. At the time of the interview, Mr. Crump had just secured coveted Disney music and used in a Gatorade commercial which played in earnest during FIFA 2014. This was a feat unimaginable for a rapper from Jackson, Mississippi, and former Southern University SGA president, but it was a challenge met successfully by Mr. Crump's unrelenting and versatile pursuit.

Some argue that following your passion is easier said than done. However not one of the over 40 Southern Greats

I interviewed presented that argument. Instead, they all presented their trials and triumphs as validation that they were consistent passion pursuers.

Following your passion can be hard to do if you don't clearly understand why you are doing it. Without your purpose defined, you will commit to a work, a career, a project only because of the expectations of others, when in actuality it was never something you were passionate about. Many people pursue a profession that is often not their passion, yet they pursue it anyway. This usually happens because they are focused on what others want them to be. This can hold true for college students, who pursue a major only because it was what their father or mother pursued and their grandfather or grandmother before them, and that student can't see him or herself doing anything different because of the family's expectation. Sometimes we find ourselves exploring options that are convenient or the options that are most readily seen. But, your purpose is important and critical to society. Therefore, you owe it to yourself and the rest of us to identify your purpose and pursue it with an unrelenting passion.

When I look back at my life, I realize that I was guilty of not following my true passion and not doing what I truly loved. I'd spent years in a major, mechanical engineering, that I didn't enjoy. As I look back at my years at Southern University and majoring in mechanical engineering, it was the other classes, serving as student government president, volunteering and working in the local community that I often found the most pleasures. See I had to keep good grades in mechanical engineering in order to continue to enjoy and operate around my passion. I would work hard class after class and would go on and graduate, but it would take another twenty-three years before I would answer the call to move into my passion perimeter. The passion perimeter is that zone where what we are called to do as our purpose and what we enjoy doing as our passion intersect. It is that zone where a job becomes play, and where you can't seem to sleep because you are so engulf in the excitement of your work. When you are living and serving your purpose, you can't help but be passionate.

    I was often guilty of coasting through life because I was not operating in my passion perimeter. When my passion and purpose called me, I would often look at the caller ID and see "caller unknown," because I didn't recognize the passion that was beckoning me. I would not answer; instead, I would continue to coast through my situations. Needless to say, this didn't produce any positive, lifelong results. What I needed to do was recognize what my passion was and pursue it with a focused vision.

    It wasn't as if I was void of great examples of people who had followed their passions. I have had many examples of great leaders who have all followed their passions and answered their call. I've had many mentors whose words of wisdom I can never forget. However, in order for passion to be pursued, gaining wisdom from great examples is not enough; it must be followed by action.

As you read through this chapter, you will see how Southern Greats thrived when they answered their calling and truly operated in their passion perimeter.

Pursuing Their Passions

As I sat in the Third Ward of Houston, Texas, interviewing **Rev. Leslie Smith,** I listened to him talk about his passion for helping people in need. A glow of pride instantly spread across his face. He vividly described his dream of buying crack houses and helping underprivileged people. At the time that this true calling was beckoning him, Rev. Smith was doing well in his corporate job at Kroger Grocery where he was responsible for fully stocking new, empty grocery stores as the company expanded. Then, he'd be responsible for hiring all new employees for the location. This was a high profile and highly desirable position within Kroger. It was also a very demanding job. Rev. Smith did his job very well, however, it was passion that was calling him and his passion was to help others. This caused Rev. Smith to leave Kroger's and start a trek into the non-profit arena.

Rev. Smith shared with me how God places the pieces together in our lives in order to help us carry out our true calling and purpose. He told me about 70-year-old

Claudine Henderson who taught him how to successfully pursue and manage grants and other types of funding for non-profits. Her advice helped him to win his first grant and since he has raised millions in funding for Change Happens!, his Houston-based 27,000-square-foot outreach center. He was able to accomplish this within the first eleven years of operation. Rev. Smith, who'd earned a bachelor's degree in marketing and management at Southern, was enthusiastic about going right out to the communities and helping them, but he knew he would have acted in haste. He knew he first needed some advice from someone who knew non-profit business development. Claudine Henderson was that mentor.

He said the opportunity to meet her was a sign for him to proceed following his desire to impact undeserved citizens in the Third Ward. "When you are following your true calling, God becomes obligated to provide you with resources to succeed," he said.

I agree.

We are never alone in following our passions; there is always a person or a particular situation that God provides to enable us to pursue our passions. What we need to do is recognize those resources and then utilize them—all while keeping your purpose and dream clearly in mind.

Rev. Smith is a perfect example. He was initially planning on building an 18,000-square-foot building, however, he felt that a building that size was too small for the vision and for the work he would complete. His decision is an example that when we are pursuing our passion, we must think bigger and hold ourselves to the larger vision. You have to see your dream bigger than what you first dreamed it could be. Rev. Smith knew that there were thousands of other people in many different communities that would benefit from his organization. So, he envisioned a bigger building and allowed his passion to fuel what he had conceived.

By doing this, Rev. Smith was unknowing following the advice of motivational business leader Zig Ziglar who said, "When obstacles arise, you change your direction to reach your goal, you do not change your decision to get there."

As Rev. Smith moved forward in his decision, the additional resources that he needed to build a larger building just seemed to appear, he said. Now, Change Happens! houses more than fifty full-time employees all serving the community. It has grown from one program to eighteen programs that now reach out to more than five school districts and thousands of students on a weekly basis.

When I asked Rev. Smith if he was satisfied with his life now and the accomplishments of Change Happens!, he reached over and pulled out the drawings for Phase II of the Change Happens! complex which will house entrepreneurs and serve as a job-training center. Once again, he's thinking bigger. Once completed, Phase II of Change Happens! will allow start-up businesses to operate side-by-side with non-profit organizations and enable them to get start growing successful operations. Change Happens!'s purpose is to educate the residents of Houston and empower them to pursue their own goals and develop their own passions. Rev. Smith wants them to know assuredly that change can happen for them. He is passion-driven, carrying an inner drive that many people can't fully comprehend. His passion continues to propel him forward towards new dreams and reaching vast levels of success. With that, though, he points out, "Your true calling may not make your rich, but it will definitely enrich your life."

Those three words from him—"enrich your life"—floats in my mind as I write and work to complete this book within the constraints of other deadlines and pressing goals. His words force me to reflect on the accomplishments I've made as a result of following my passion of coaching business owners while developing Top Choice Promotions, my advertising promotions company. Those accomplishments truly have not made me rich but the lessons within each passion pursuit have enriched my life.

I can't continue discussing passion without mentioning Dennis S. Brown also known as *Mr. Attitude*. Mr. Brown is a well-known motivational speaker who certainly knows a lot about pursuing passion. Although he is now in the business of motivating people to pursue their passions with positive attitudes, he wasn't always in this line of work. Prior to becoming a motivational speaker, Mr. Brown was working comfortably as an accountant for an international oil company in Houston, Texas. Then, he decided to take a massive faith leap and transform into a successful motivational speaker. As an accountant, Mr. Brown would calculate numbers on a daily basis and focus on how those numbers related to the corporation's success. It did not require much interaction with people. Becoming a motivational speaker was a complete contrast. It requires Mr. Brown to develop relationships with people on a daily basis and deduce methods and ways for them to be encouraged to change their lives. This transformation demanded that Mr. Brown dedicate his focus on human response not numerical reactions.

    I wanted to know more about why Dennis "Mr. Attitude" Brown chose to become a motivational speaker. When I asked him, he began to talk about how the words of key people, such as Les Brown and Zig Ziglar, helped him get through a difficult stretch of ten years in his life when he lost his father, two brothers, and two sisters.

    "The words that they spoke helped get me through those rough spots and grow to become a better person," he said. "I knew then that I wanted to be a person who could give that to others and help them with through their rough spots in life." From his difficult circumstances, Mr. Brown coined the mantra that he is now known for: ***The difference between a good day and bad day is your attitude!***

Changing careers with "following a passion" as the sole reason for that change was not an easy transition for Mr. Brown. (It oftentimes isn't any for many people). Many times he only had his relationship with God to rely on, and the encouraging words that mentors poured into his life throughout the years kept him on his passion pursuit and within his passion perimeter. It was during the trying times that he would have to remind himself that he wanted to help people through spoken, motivational words and not with numbers and spreadsheets. He had to constantly remind himself that he could offer the world more with his life now as a speaker than he could as an accountant.

When he first made the move towards his passion, people around him told him he was crazy for leaving a stable and reliable job. They even questioned how he was going to feed his family. Little did they know that he was so passion-driven that he would wake up every morning and deliver newspapers to support his family and make sure that his daughters didn't miss their dance lessons. (In fact, at the 2012 Super Bowl his baby girl danced with Madonna during the halftime performance.)

When you are pursuing your passion, the innate fuel you need will surface and boil inside of you, giving you extra momentum to endure and continue on—especially during the hardest of times.

Like the other Southern Greats, Mr. Brown faced doubts, criticism, and isolation but still pressed toward success. About that, Mr. Brown said profoundly, "You have to be careful with whom you share your dreams." People will always have their opinions and some will have negative reactions to the things we passionately pursue, but we must develop thick skin and an inner confidence in order to see passion come to fruition. In the end, it is not anyone else's journey to walk out but our own.

Mr. Brown has gone from having to throw newspapers to support his passion to having multi-national companies including ExxonMobil, McDonald's, and Chevron routinely pay for him to motivate employees and leaders.

Passion helped him commit to taking a leap of faith and following his dream. Now, that passion drives him daily to continue helping people change their attitudes, their lives, and the lives of those around them.

Another Southern Great who knows firsthand the benefits of being within their passion perimeter is Dexter Henderson, a senior executive with IBM. Mr. Henderson stepped in his passion perimeter early on in his career at IBM. For as long as he could remember, he always had a strong desire to know how things worked, especially technology. Mr. Henderson "always wanted to know the newest and the greatest. This love and quest to know has taken me all over the world during my career at IBM." He has passionately worked in the technology field for more than thirty years and has helped bring about important change in people's lives through it.

His love, his passion for technology pulled him away from the football fields of the Houston Gamblers, a United States Football League (USFL) team, when he had to choose between a playing a professional sport or being a technology professional. I imagined this being a tough decision for him.

But it wasn't. He simply said, "I always knew that working in technology and helping the world from that vantage point was what I wanted to do and to be." So when he had to choose between IBM and professional football at the age of 22, the call was rather easy because he understood his purpose and knew what he loved to do.

By operating in his passion perimeter, Mr Henderson has traveled the world and worked in more than fifty countries. Even today, he wakes up every morning excited about working in technology.

When I think about the significance of pursuing your true calling, I am immediately drawn to the testimony of Rev. Byron Stevenson who believed he was a person called to serve the Lord in ministry. Since knowing what his true calling in life was, Rev. Stevenson has pursued it wholeheartedly. He also didn't disregard the significance of the lessons he learned leading up to him growing his ministry. "We are the sum total of all our life experiences," he said.

That statement alone wasn't enough for me. I was intrigued and wanted to know more so I asked him to explain. He said God knew that he would need his Southern University accounting degree when he would be called to start and lead The Fort Bend Church in the spring of 2004.

Just before taking the position at The Fort Bend Church, Rev. Stevenson gave up an associate pastor position at one of Houston's most prominent mega-churches. A position at a mega-church would have been the ideal ticket to ensuring that he would work in the ministry and fully provide for his family. However, he knew that he had to go where he was truly called and where he was most passionate. Taking this new position (which laid squarely within his passion perimeter) meant that he would have to get an additional job to provide for his family and so that the new church would not have to try and support him before it was able. This was where his accounting degree proved to be essential. He was able to quickly get an accounting position in order to support his family and ultimately do the work he was purposed to do.

Rev. Stevenson's first church service was on August 1, 2004, in a local school gymnasium. This setting didn't hinder nor discouraged his passion for the ministry or the people he was serving. He knew that no matter where they had services, the move of God was not going to be limited. To his surprise, more than 600 worshippers attended that first service, and 300 people became members. Because of his passion, Rev. Stevenson has grown the church membership to more than 5,000 members and has been recognized nationally as one of the fastest growing congregations in the country. They are no longer in that local gymnasium where they began, and Rev. Stevenson no longer has to maintain a second job to help support his family. With all this success, Rev. Stevenson still maintains he will never forget his humble beginnings. So, don't be distracted by the large congregation that The Fort Bend Church now has; Rev. Stevenson isn't. He quickly reminded me that it's not about the large numbers, but about the small numbers. It's the small numbers that represent each and every individual who is a member. All of these individuals make up the entire church of people that Rev. Stevenson serves every day. What really matters, he said, are the numbers of lives that are touched daily and the numbers of families that the Fort Bend Church is able to impact in and around Sugarland, Texas. Additionally, the small things that the church is able to do within the community will have a lasting affect not the number of committed members.

Let's continue with another Southern Great who also pursued his passion, stayed within his passion perimeter, and found enduring fulfillment.

Dr. Warren Valdry followed his passion of architecture and made a fortune developing real estate. Of course I was curious. So, I asked how was he able to amass such a fortune by doing what he loved, and he pointed out a couple of things to me. He said, "One. This is what I was trained by Southern (University) to do. Two, the niche that I filled served a need and helped others; and three, I developed a process and I began to teach it to others."

Dr. Valdry had a passion, knew what he had to do to pursue it, and worked hard to ensure that it happened. He wasn't pursuing a fortune, he was pursuing his true calling. He was working in his passion perimeter. And through this calling, he was able to provide a valuable service to others. Dr. Valdry was able to take his Southern University training and strategically place homes and developments in the fast growing areas of Los Angeles, California. "I not only thought horizontal, I also so thought vertical. I was able to creatively maximize the use of properties. This all start with my love and my passion to build and help others," he said.

When you look at the fortune that Dr. Valdry and his brother have been able to earn you could easily assume their work has been about the money. However, as you look at the organizations they support with their time and money, you will quickly realize that they worked so passionately so that they could help and serve others on a great level.

The more I talked with Southern Greats, the more I see a consistent character trait among them. They are passion-driven and willing to serve in the most meaningful ways.

Bishop Joseph Walker enrolled in Southern University as an English major preparing for a career as an attorney. He jokingly explained that "law was the family business." Being the youngest in his family, he has several siblings that are attorneys and even a judge. So he had purposely planned to be an attorney, however during his senior year in college he received his calling to go into ministry. In 1992, at the age of 24, Bishop Walker began his pastorate at Mt. Zion Baptist Church in Nashville, Tennessee, with 175 members. The ministry has grown to more than 28,000 members and continues to grow at a phenomenal rate of nearly 1,800 members annually. Under Bishop Walker's leadership, Mt. Zion has expanded beyond its original location in the Historic Jefferson Street Corridor to seven weekly services in three physical locations and includes an online ministry at www.mtzionanywhere.org, its fourth church location, and an intense social media presence. In April 2006, his leadership also expanded to Jackson, Tennessee, where the Zion Church became the first church plant of Mt. Zion Baptist Church.

Bishop Walker's answering of this calling has taken him from the English department at Southern University to the presiding Bishop-elect of the Full Gospel Baptist Church Fellowship International.

I would argue that Bishop Walker would have been a highly successful attorney. However by answering his true calling and following his true purpose, he impacts hundreds of thousands of lives on a monthly basis through the various media of his ministries.

This is ultimately the goal of your success: *to think beyond yourself and help someone else.*

I could sense Southern Great **Felicia Conley** smiling through the phone as she thought about how much she actually enjoys her job and enjoys getting up to go to work every morning. "I love to solve problems and develop technical mastery," said Ms. Conley who is a plant manager at Procter and Gamble's Tampax factory in Maine. Her career has enabled her to not only pursue her passion, but also help to solve problems. Isn't it fulfilling to know that your passion and your profession can go hand-in-hand?

As a plant manager at P&G, Ms. Conley has a hefty responsibility to oversee the day-to-day function and maintenance of the facility. Her commitment to her responsibilities and passion is more than appreciated, and she is reaping the rewards of passionately pursuing her goals.

This leads me to talk about **Cleo Fields**, a Southern Great and former Louisiana congressman. On the day I interviewed Mr. Fields, he was preparing for football season and watching engineers install new parts for the Doug Williams Stadium at the Louisiana Leadership Institute in Baton Rouge. (The Leadership Institute is a state of the art complex that also includes the stadium, the Avery Johnson Gymnasium, and the Debbie Allen Performing Arts Center.)

From the stadium's press box, I watch Mr. Fields in action—manifesting his passion. I reminded myself that following your passion, relentlessly, was not new for him. He has gone from the classrooms on Southern University's campus, through the reigns of the Louisiana Legislature and Congress, and now to the creation of the Louisiana Leadership Institution.

He smiled as he pointed out in front of him and said, "Look at this field, stadium, and other facilities here at the Louisiana Leadership Institute. All of this was born out of my passion to help underprivileged kids to be exposed to something different and something positive."

He said the Institute was birthed out of a collaboration of many great people within the community coming together to serve others.

When you look closely at the career of this former US Congressman, you will realize that he is where he is today because he chose to pursue his purpose of serving others in 1987 while in law school at Southern University Law Center. As a 24-year-old law student, Mr. Fields decided to run against a well-established incumbent Louisiana State Senator. He went on to win this election and served as one the youngest state senators in the country. He later was elected to serve in the U.S. House of Representative from 1993-1997.

When I asked him why did he chose to run for public office versus continue into his career as an attorney. He simply said he knew his purpose in life was to help other young men and women have opportunities to change and have better lives. He continues this mission and purpose through the work of the Louisiana Leadership Institute.

The path of these Southern Greats demonstrate that following your passion can take you many places: from IBM, to ministry, to management, to the football stadium, and even to the recording studio. I had the pleasure of interviewing a well-known name in the music industry and a Southern Great **Lavell Crump**. Known in the industry as David Banner, Mr. Crump is a platinum-selling rapper and music producer from Jackson, Mississippi.

"I always knew that I wanted to be a music performer and producer. It was my mom who said I needed to go to college. I can remember her taking me to Southern. Since we had not preregistered there was not a place for me in the system so we had to wait. However, she was persistent in getting me enrolled into school… and she did. This experience showed me firsthand how powerful passion combined with persistence is. I have used this lesson many times in my life to help me breakthrough new territories," he said.

His expertise and unrelenting passion propels him to pursue what he loves: music; but it is his persistence to stay within his passion perimeter that has taken him exactly to where he wanted to be in the industry. And, as I shared earlier, his commitment to honoring his purpose has led him to branch beyond the hip-hop music industry and into big screen film and commercial productions.

As I close this chapter on following your passion, let me share with you the thoughts of the **Rev. Ladell Graham**. Rev. Graham has chosen to truly live in his passion perimeter. He was co-founder and partner at Smith Graham, one of the largest minority, fixed-asset management firms in the country. This firm manages billion dollar investment portfolios for various well-known Fortune 100 companies and municipalities. Rev. Graham was living the world of high finance and worldwide investments, until he decided to walk away and work in ministry.

Can you image the conversation he had with himself? Assuredly, this was not an easy decision.

As I sat in Rev. Graham's home in Sugarland, Texas, he said he knew making the decision to leave Smith Graham was something that he had to do. At this time, Rev. Graham was not a pastor of a church, he just knew that he was born to minister; he was born to serve the Lord and to serve mankind.

Believing that becoming a minister was his true calling, Rev. Graham would sell his interest in the company to his partner and begin volunteering fulltime with the Abundant Life Christian Center. What a commitment to your calling!

I asked Rev. Graham to share with me insight that would help a person to seek and move toward their true purpose passionately. As a minister and national speaker, Rev. Graham often speaks to groups about what he refers to as P3: potential, passion, purpose. When I pressed him for the abbreviated version of his speech, he summarized it as:

1. Potential is that non-performing asset we all have within us.
2. Passion is that God-given fuel and desire to solve the problem that we were born to address.
3. Purpose (you guessed it) is that problem we were born to solve.

As I left his home on that Friday afternoon, I could not stop thinking about all of the non-performing assets (all the potential) that I was personally sitting on. How many of us live life and don't use our potential. Once we start to move from the position of potential toward purpose I truly believe that it will ignite our true passion. When you are pursuing your goals, your objectives, and your purpose with passion you are unstoppable. If you don't move away from the potential position, you will never bless the world with your true gift; your true purpose.

Before you stop or move on to the next chapter, I challenge you to work through the "Reflections from the Bluff" section below.

DO IT NOW!

REFLECTIONS FROM THE BLUFF

What is YOUR purpose in life?

_____
_____
_____
_____

What would you be doing if you knew with certainty that you could not fail?

1._____
_____
_____

2._____
_____
_____

3._____
_____

How will the world benefit from you following your purpose and operating in your passion perimeter?

_____
_____
_____
_____

BEING A TRENDSETTER... BEING A TRAILBLAZER

The words trendsetter and trailblazer are words that I always associate with bravery, boldness, and confidence. And rightly so. Those who wear these titles should wear them proudly.

History has a way of remembering and recognizing trailblazers and trendsetters. Often they are not remembered and recognized until long after they are retired, been removed, or have passed away. Usually, most trendsetters and trailblazers do not set out to do something memorable. Instead, what they have in mind is what they consider to be a necessary goal, dream, or vision. However, somewhere in between chasing and exceeding that goal they become recognized as a trendsetter and a trailblazer for those coming behind them and travelling in their footsteps.

So, what exactly are trendsetters and trailblazers? Well, the official definitions are:

- **Trendsetter** — one who initiates or popularizes a trend

- **Trailblazer** — a leader or pioneer in a particular field

As I sit on Scott's Bluff, the beautiful levee at the back of the Southern University campus, I watch a tugboat push a load up the mighty Mississippi River.

I think about how as humans, we often find ourselves in the middle of the river of life and, at some point, we have the choice of going with the flow or we can choose to be the trendsetter and go against the waves.

I think about what it takes to go against the current, to be different, to go against the flow. It takes being willing to go against the status quo currents much like the powerful tugboats that push thousands of tons of products against the currents of the mighty Mississippi River. It takes being different and courageous. It takes being a visionary and trendsetter.

Being different doesn't mean that you are a trendsetter. But in order to be trendsetter, you have to be different. I truly believe trendsetters are just ordinary people who made the choice to live their life by occasionally going against the current. Trendsetters chose to give the extra effort required for going against strong currents.

When I look closely at the tugboat, I remember that it takes significantly more fuel for it to go against the current and travel up river than for it to travel and float peacefully with the current.

The first Southern Great I will feature in this chapter was setting trends and blazing a trail throughout higher education in a most remarkably talented way. He is the late Dr. Issac Greggs, former band director of Southern University's marching band, the Human Jukebox, which was the first HBCU band in the nation to synchronize the steps of more than 150 members to the music they performed on the field. Doc, as he is affectionately called by many Southern alumni, has always been about being better. Any of the hundreds of men and women who earned the opportunity to march with the Human Jukebox know this famous quote from Doc: *"You can't be as good as; You must be better than"*.

I had the opportunity to interview Doc for this book before his passing in 2014 where I asked him what he meant by his famous quote. He explained to me that he never wanted to be considered the same as someone else, he wanted to be better than everyone else. He talked about how he would breakdown and critique his own show just to make himself better. This is the thought process of a trendsetter: *Do not desire to be like anyone else, but be different and even better than everyone else.* Trendsetters are not carbon copies of what or who is popular at the time. Rather, they create the trends that others will follow and imitate.

After sitting together watching a couple of hours of Southern University halftime shows, I asked Doc what was it that earned him and the Human Jukebox the recognition it has as the number one show band in America. He smiled and told me that it was because of commitment. He explained more and began talking about the many hours that his band members would practice to get one song down to perfection and that was just practicing to perfect their sound. After they got the music down, then it was time to hit the field to get the precision of the steps and moves. Once they mastered both the music and the steps to perfection, it was time to repeat it all over again. The constant practice and repetition is what made them excellent. Once it came time for them to perform, they solidified why the nation saw the SU Human Jukebox Marching Band as the best and why Doc Greggs was a trendsetter.

    Doc also said that when he thinks of a trendsetter, he thinks of someone who often pushes the envelope or even breaks the rules. After he left Southern University and retired, he was tapped to work with and lead The Louisiana Leadership Institute All-Star Marching Band. Greggs lead the band whose members were high school student to perform in the Rose Bowl Parade, one of the most prestigious honors for any marching unit. At the time, the Pasadena Tournament of Roses Association had a policy that prohibited bands from stopping in the streets and performing a marching routine for the viewing stand. Being the trailblazer that he was Doc "forget" this rule and had his leadership band stop in front of the judges' stand and do a complete unsolicited routine where the members performed and positioned themselves to form R-O-S-E in the middle of the street.

Needless to say, the leadership band was offered a standing invitation to future Rose Parades. This bold move turned out to be beneficial for the band in the end. This trendsetting performance and attitude caused the parade committee to change the rules around bands performing a routine. That is what trendsetters and trailblazers do: They break the rules but also changing the game.

This brings a up a great point about trendsetter. Trendsetters must being willing to bend and sometimes break the existing rules or change status quo. As I explored Doctor Greggs life I realized that this was one of the most common trait to his successes. Dr. Greggs was always willing to be different and set new trends. So I challenge you to not look at things as they are; look at things as they may be and then begin to work and be a difference maker in every situation of your life.

Another Southern Great and trendsetter is president of the Siemens Foundation, Jeniffer Harper-Taylor, whose duties falls right into what she is most passionate about: changing how women and minorities participate in science, technology, engineering, and math fields. At a quick glance, her background would show her to be one of the most unlikely candidates for making such a change. She was a mass communications major looking to pursue a career in public relations and marketing. However, life's circumstances caused Mrs. Harper-Taylor to go from PR to HR, then to the STEM department. This is where she began to make her mark in helping the next generation of scientists and engineers.

As the Foundation's president, Mrs. Harper-Taylor's primary responsibility is to develop new and innovative programs that will stimulate and challenge today's minority STEM students. She has spearheaded programs including the Siemens' We Can Change the World Challenge, which encourages K-12 students to develop innovative green solutions for environmental issues. Such initiatives have lead Mrs. Harper-Taylor to be recognized on *The Network Journal*'s fourteenth annual list of "25 Influential Black Women in Business" and most recently she was profiled in a salute to the extraordinary STEM leadership of women across all sectors in the book, *100 Women Leaders in STEM*. She is also routinely interviewed by **U.S. News & World Report, the Washington Post, the Los Angeles Times,** and Bloomberg Radio.

If a trailblazer is a leader in a particular field, then the founder of MPN Portal, CJ Bland, is certainly a trailblazer. MPN Portal is a national portal that provides technology and tools for major corporations to recruit professional minorities. When you talk with this man from the inner city of New Orleans, you won't see the physics degree from Dillard University or the electrical engineering degree from Southern University. Instead, you see a humble man with a passion for finding new and innovative ways of bringing professionals together. His portal helps to provide resources for corporations and job opportunities for individuals. It's a win-win situation.

His search for win-win situation and to provide a needed service began as local newsletter and lead to one of the first web portals that focused on employment opportunities for minorities. Imagine what it took to step out and row against the current to make such product useful, beneficial and profitable tool. By choosing to do things different, Mr. Bland has help hundreds of thousands of professionals find better career opportunities and better employment.

Mr. Bland found a unique blend of filing a service void and creating opportunities for others. That is a mark of a true trendsetter. The late Dr. Emmit Bashful, the first chancellor of Southern University of New Orleans in 1956, operated in the same vein as a higher education trendsetter. When I ask Dr. Bashful what was it like to be the first president of a start-up university. Ironically, he did not speak of the challenges that he faced. He didn't speak of the lack of resources and the meager facilities. He spoke of the opportunity he had to create a Black middle class in New Orleans. As I sat in front of Dr. Bashful with a perplexed look on my face, he begin to explain, "It was my desire and mission at Southern University New Orleans to provide the opportunity for working class individuals to earn a bachelor's degree and thereby create new opportunities for them and their families. This often meant that we had to try things in education that were not common in 1950s ." Dr. Bashful saw it as his purpose and role to help reverse the directions and open new opportunities for Blacks in New Orleans. He became recognized as one of few people who helped to shape and change the landscape of New Orleans—especially for Black residents.

Oftentimes, new trends and new trendsetters are born out of simply asking the question how can I do it differently? How can I make it different? Or how can I change and not follow the status quos?

Remember, Vincent Scott Lyons from the previous chapters? He's another trendsetter. In his mid-thirties he was selected as the Vice President of Engineering and Product Development for the Maytag Corporation. When he was appointed, the Maytag refrigeration division was facing lagging sales, and he sought out new trends in order to turn that department around. I asked Mr. Lyons how he was able to do it, and he said, "I knew that I would have to challenge my team to make Maytag the strongest and best in the marketplace. In order to be the best we would have to develop new products and concepts. This led to the development of the French door concept for refrigerators.

The target sales amount for the first year was 30,000 units and we were able to sell 150,000 units in the first year."

These are truly impressive numbers. Mr. Lyons helped to set an industry trend for the Maytag refrigeration company and in turn helped to increase profits. Today, the French-door refrigerators are standard across multiple manufactors. In fact, you may have one in your home right now. If so, thank Southern Great Vincent Lyons for that Maytag-first development.

"I live for the opportunity to create a new platform and new products," he said.

Mr. Vincent Lyons is a trendsetter and a difference maker.

Greg Baranco became a trendsetter at a very early age. I had the opportunity to sit down with Mr. Baranco at his Mercedes of Buckhead car dealership. As a trailblazer, Mr. Baranco was one of the first, Black man to integrate Baton Rouge's all-male Catholic High School. He learned from this trying experience that he could achieve anything if he chose to be unique. Mr. Baranco pulled from this experience and became a Baton Rouge trendsetter when he decided to be a new car salesman at Mid City Ford in 1969. Now, you must understand that in 1969, it was not common to see Blacks selling new cars anywhere in the city of Baton Rouge. Mr. Baranco turned many heads when they saw him walk into Mid City Ford. He would share with me how he convinced the General Manager to give him the opportunity to sale new cars (his first sale). However after the trial period he didn't quite live up to the standards. But because of his work ethic the top salesperson at the dealership took a liking to Mr. Baranco (second sale) and agreed to take him under his wing. With this personal mentor and his drive and work ethic, Mr. Baranco would go on to become the General Manager of this dealership prior to owning his first dealership.

When I asked him what made him successful as one of the first Black car salesperson and new car auto dealer in the Deep South, he said, "I do not focus on what I don't know. I focus on what I know, and no matter what the situation is I can out work anyone. I also believe that it is important to learn new things."

If you ever have the opportunity to visit Mr. Baranco's Mercedes dealership in Atlanta you will see various example of a trendsetters mindset. The first one is in the service lanes of his dealership. When a customer pull up their picture and name is displayed on flat screen monitor and simultaneously the customer's assigned sale representative is paged to alert the salesperson that one of their customers in the building. Another example is the facility itself. Most dealerships are spread over open areas but not Mr. Baranco's Mercedes of Buckhead which is located in a four-story complex. I ask Mr. Baranco why he invested in such a unique structure, and he simply said, "this allows us to house all of our cars in a garage. You don't buy a Mercedes to park it outside." These are just part of the reasons Mr. Baranco's dealership has won Mercedes' award for top dealership in service and just part of the reasons his dealership grossed more than $150 million in sales.

No matter what your profession, you must seek to start trends and be different than others. As Mr. Baranco said, "you must always ask yourself how can you do things differently and serve others. By doing this, you will always become a better person and add value to your employees, clients, and community."

Another great example is Dr. Rani Whitfield. As a practicing physician known as "Da' Hip Hop Doc," Dr. Whitfield has a love and passion for communicating strategies for good health to people, especially to young people. He is a trendsetter who packages his health-conscious messages within the rhymes of hip-hop and within the vivid images of his four-book comic collection. As I interviewed Dr. Whitfield, he told me that he was from a family of musicians which gave him an edge to set a new trend. One day, he took an old rap song and worked the beat around the message of good health. He noticed how responsive youth were and that made him crank up the creative side. Dr. Whitfield then went from a local doctor speaking in community centers in Baton Rouge to a nationally recognized crusader of health. No other doctors were merging health and rap music—and very few do so today.

Since his popularity has grown, Da' Hip Hop Doc has made appearances on the Tom Joyner Morning Show, CNN, the Michael Baisden show, and Louisiana Public Broadcasting. You can even catch him and his band, U4Ria, rocking the room at many venues throughout the state. Dr. Whitfield is definitely going against the current and as a result, he is creating his own unique path and brand that makes him successful in the examination room and on the stage.

Trailblazer. Trendsetter. Difference maker. All these titles describe who Bishop Joseph Walker III has been for the city of Nashville. A true trendsetter, Bishop Walker has set himself apart to do something that no one has attempted to do before because of his love and passion. He graduated from Southern University in a little more than three years, and then graduated as the youngest Black to get a doctor of ministry degree from Princeton Theological Seminary. At the age of 24, he became pastor of a 175-member church and grew it to more than 28,000 members.

If you look closely at Bishop Walker, you will realize how he has become such a trailblazer, such a great leader, and such a great servant. Bishop Walker has been one of the first pastors to totally embrace the digital world. Just go to www.moutzionanywhere.com. The dynamic site not only allows you to view streaming services, it truly allows people all over the world to experience Mt. Zion in real time. Bishop Walker could have stopped there. But that is not what trailblazers do. They continue to blaze trails that will help them achieve and fulfill their purpose. This is evident by Bishop Walker's use of mobile apps, prayer line conference calls, and timely books about worldly relevant issues and topics.

The mark of a trendsetter is found in the person's willingness to go the extra mile and stand out above others. When Milton Scott came to the Arthur Anderson accounting firm, there were no Black partners. He became the first. To make partner in the Big Six accounting firm, you had to be in the top 2% to 3% ranking of accountants. Mr. Scott endured long work hours and late nights of sometimes sleeping in his office under his desk in order to reach his goals within the firm.

Mr. Scott shared several thoughts that are critical to be a top business person and trendsetter, "First, the individual must realize that all partners are not created equal. Secondly, you must be part of the culture and learn what is needed to be part of it. Third, you must continuously develop yourself and be serving your community. And lastly, you must be constantly asking yourself what do I do to differentiate myself from others."
Mr. Scott has always been a trendsetter and truly a difference maker in everything he has chosen to pursue. When he decided to leave Corporate America as the Chief

Administrative Officer of a Fortune 500 company, Dynegy, in 2002 he became a managing director at The StoneCap Group LP. The company acquires power generation assets. In 2004 with three partners, Mr. Scott formed Complete Energy Partners, LLC, a start-up investment firm that purchases power plants. Their work involves raising capital, arranging financing, and using the relationships the partners have built over the years to "open doors with sellers," he said. "Our first deal was a $330 million dollar transaction. If I had not been prepared to do this because of all of my previous work, no one would take us seriously. I'm taking on a lot more risk; but quite frankly I am not nervous. I am quite comfortable with what I can do."

As Co-Founder, Managing Director, and CFO of Complete Energy Holdings, LLC, a company he began in order to acquire, own, and operate power generation assets in the United States. He co-led two successful acquisitions. The first acquisition was the 837-megawatt Batesville Generating Facility in Batesville, Miss., acquired in August 2004 for $330 million. The second acquisition was the 1,022-megawatt La Paloma Generating Facility near Bakersfield, Calif., acquired for $580 million in August 2005. This acquisition, hailed by Project Finance International as "the power deal of the year," included private equity, mezzanine debt, and first and second lien project financed debt.

As you look at a snapshot of Mr. Scott's bio, you will see that he has always been one to take a chance. None is more evident than his work with the TAOS GROUP, founded in 2007. The TAOS GROUP has grown to be a well-respected international firm in the energy and supply chain management. I asked Milton about the TAOS GROUP expansion into the African Market and simply stated that is where significant growth opportunities are. After stating a variety of statistics about the growth potential over the continent of Africa, he said, "being there now will give us an opportunity to make a difference."

Consistent in the characteristics of these greats is that their actions and attitude to be excellent has set them apart in every capacity. Like them, you must be willing to chart, explore, and conquer new territory.

REFLECTIONS FROM THE BLUFF:

What is your definition of being a trendsetter?

_____
_____
_____
_____

What are three ways that you can set new trends in your current market, industry or company?

1. _____
   _____
   _____
   _____

2. _____
   _____
   _____
   _____

3. _____
   _____
   _____
   _____

When and what is the next time you will do something for the first time?

_____
_____

MOTIVATION AND SELF-DETERMINATION

You have heard various phrases about the lack of motivation. From "he or she lacks the motivation or the drive to push forward" or "they lack the motivation to be successful" to "he or she lacks motivation to earn good grades or to be a star athlete or performer." Then, there are the statements that the person lacks the motivation to write that best-selling book or create that play or record that song. These are not words that someone neither wants to hear nor wants to say about someone else.

Everyone has within them an innate need to accomplish a goal or dream; to be motivated to do something and be someone successful. As I researched the subject of motivation, the last phrase about being motivated to write that best-selling book really hit home with me as I thought of my own motivation in completing this book on the Southern Greats.

My goal was simple. I wanted to give Southern University alumni a platform to describe their joyful moments at Southern and tell of the lessons they learned that empowered them to be successful. I was determined to succeed in my goal of writing this book.

Determination was my first step. However, determination by itself was not enough. There had to be some development or, let me be totally honest, there had to be *a lot* of development in order to bring the idea of a book about the legacy of Southern University through its alumni to fruition. As I now look at this process, I am aware of how self-motivation is developed over time and with focused determination. It is a two-step process. First, the individual must set or define their purpose. This purpose can be anything, any goal or dream. The key is to define what your purpose is and why you want to accomplish it. The second step is to have some development. Basically, the individual must have a plan to see their purpose or goal accomplished. This plan can be a written outline or meetings you've organized with someone to help you get started on your goal. It involves looking within yourself, assessing your strengths and identifying the tools you already possess to propel you forward.

For me to accomplish the goal of compiling interviews from three dozen alumni and produce a book, it took me realizing that I already had relationships with many of them to one degree or another. That was a major tool already in my grasp. I also have a determined spirit that allowed me to ask what I needed from one alumnus in order to connect with another and another until I reached my goal. That strategy, that technique, of speaking up and requesting interviews propelled this project. I was positioned to thrust forward once I took the time to really reflect, think through, and utilize what I already had in my hand to pursue this purpose—to accomplish this task.

Having grown up in a household where both my dad and Grandpa where building contractors, I had the opportunity to understand development in one of the simplest forms: through building houses. Building a house doesn't just happen. It starts with a blueprint. By having this blueprint, completing the task and achieving the goal is made a lot easier and a lot more attainable.

When I think about a person who had a clear life blueprint, I think again to Mr. Milton Scott. In the early '80s, as part of Arthur Anderson and after deciding to pursue his goal of becoming a partner, Mr. Scott realized that all partners were not created equal. He focused on what he could offer to the firm based on his strengths and attributes. Then, he determined that he would be a valuable asset to the firm. He strategically mapped out his strengths to help him to stay motivated. This motivation pushed him to spend countless hours working for his clients. It was even rumored that he would often sleep overnight at his desk. Mr. Scott's motivation to succeed coupled with the blueprint he created to showcase his strengths as an accountant, made him a shoe-in for the position of full partner.

Motivation is often defined as a person's inner drive; that little voice that tells us to get up and keep moving when all else seems impossible. There is a phrase that states, "By the yard, it is hard and by the inch, it is a cinch." Essentially, what that means is that a little effort eventually goes a long way. We must do a little bit every day to adhere to this principle. I refer to it as a principle because it is always true whether you use this principle in school by simply reviewing your class notes each day for fifteen to twenty minutes versus waiting until the night before to cram or working on that important business presentation for thirty to forty minutes each day versus waiting until the day before to complete it.

One person who embodies this principle is Dexter Henderson. When I asked him what motivates and drives him to succeed, Mr. Henderson said, "I have this drive to be perceived as the smartest person in the room. It is not being conceited it is about simply being the best." It is this type of motivation that leads him to spend fifteen minutes each day on any random topic, reading, and researching every topic. Fifteen minutes per day gives him just enough time to quickly become an expert on a subject. As an expert he becomes the smartest in the room on that subject. He knew what goal he wanted to achieve and how he needed to get there to accomplish this. Then, he created a blueprint, a plan, to achieve his purpose.

Self-motivation is a very strong attribute. When utilized in a positive way, self-motivation gives you an unstoppable drive to succeed and reach a desired point. Self-motivation not only allows you to keep moving forward, it sometimes makes you run forward when others think you are crazy or think that you are pursuing a crazy dream. Self-motivation is the intrinsic motivator that causes you to pursue your goal or dream no matter its size or ability. It is the thing that makes you stay up late at night or that makes you get up at ungodly hours in the morning. It's the thing that will not let you take "no" for answer, even if you have heard "no" ten times before. Self-motivation helps you to quiet your naysayers and slay your giants.

Another Southern Great who continuously strives for and often achieves new levels of excellence is Derrick Warren, also an executive with IBM. Even though our time was short in between international conference calls, Mr. Warren was able to share a lot about his experiences and through this dialog there were a couple of things about motivation that really stuck out with me. When I ask Mr. Warren about motivation he said, "You must be open to learning and must be willing to be a life learner that is eager and willing to learn until you die."

I asked Mr. Warren to share how he employs this principle in his life and his career. He shared with me that his desire to be a life learner is why he has numerous international experiences. His zest and zeal to continuously learn, grow, and expand his horizon have afforded him these experiences. He said he is always looking for those unique assignments that would challenge and cause him to grow.

When I asked him how does he employ the principle of continuously learning in his personal life, Mr. Warren shared with me on example from his relationship with his daughter. He said, "every month we look for some new experience to share together. We are always asking, 'When was the last time you did something for the first time?'." As I left the interview, I truly plunder the question, "when was the last time I did something for the first time?" This question will serve a person well as a motivating tool. Because as you do something for the first time, you must learn, grow, and stretch. If you seek to do it well or in excellence, you must truly learn, grow, and stretch. I would challenge you as a reader to explore and plunder what lies within your "passion perimeter" that you have not done. If you are able to develop this, you will have a motivating list to propel you through your daily challenges.

Former Congressman Cleo Fields has this type of self-motivation. Remember, in the previous chapters I wrote about interviewing him at the Doug Williams Football Stadium where he was giving orders to the construction crew to complete the stadium's bathrooms, concessions, and locker rooms prior to the opening weekend of high school football in Louisiana. He was in his element, in his passion perimeter, and he was highly motivated.

Becoming a Congressman takes a great deal of self-motivation and development. This type of self-motivation did not just begin for Mr. Fields. You can look back to his days of running for Louisiana State Senator. Mr. Fields was a 25-year-old law school student who would have to face a seasoned and well-financed incumbent. It seemed like an unwinnable challenge. However, Mr. Fields' self-motivation and self-drive made him get out on a daily basis and knock on doors asking people for their vote. It was that same self-motivation that drove him to continue to register college students to vote. And it was his self-drive that would eventually lead him to win the senate seat by 313 votes.

At the young age of 29, this same self- motivation led then Senator Fields to win a seat in the United States Congress. Mr. Fields knew that to get to Congress much would be required of him. He needed to utilize his self-motivation and his life's blueprint for his dream to become a reality.

Seeing dreams become a reality was also what happened to with Lavell "David Banner" Crump. As I sat to talk with this successful rapper and music producer, his self-motivation and determination was evident as he spoke of breaking into the entertainment industry. He shared with me some of the steps he had to take to go through the grind of learning the ins and outs of this industry. In order to be and stay relevant in the entertainment industry, Mr. Crump talked about how critical it was to learn new songs, new techniques, and new styles. By continuing to renew himself, he continues to be a popular music producer and collaborator with some of the top artists in the industry.

We can't mention self-motivation and development without also talking about self-reliance and determination. Self-reliance is defined as dependence on and confidence in one's own abilities and decisions. In order to make the best decisions for yourself or your goals, you must first believe that you can achieve success and motivate yourself to achieve it. Next, you must combine self-reliance and determination in order to do whatever is necessary to propel yourself forward and achieve that success.

When I think about self-reliance and sacrifices, I think about the sacrifices that Mr. Irving Matthews made moving from plant manager to dealership owner. Mr. Matthews was a successful plant manager with Frito Lay when he decided to apply for the Ford Motor Company's new car dealer program. Out of 300 applicants, he came through as the top applicant. Matthews shared with me how important self-growth and self-reliance was during his training period with Ford Motor Company. As a plant manager with Frito Lay, Mr. Matthews was accustomed to a certain income and lifestyle. This changed once he began his training period with Ford Motor Company. So that he would not have to subject his family to three years of financial sacrifice, he would often spend extra time studying and learning what was necessary to own and operate his own dealership. By doing this, he was able to cut the normal three years off the new dealer program to almost half. It did not just stop there. Mr. Matthews also utilized the same principles and approach when he took over his first Ford Dealership.

"When I was in the training program, I made sure that I learned how to do every aspect of the operations. I realized that the more that I could do myself, the better I could operate my own store and the quicker I could be profitable. I would not be satisfied with learning the overview and how the parts department worked; I wanted to get in and actually do the paperwork and complete the process myself." In 1991, Mr. Matthews opened his first Ford dealership. He now owns two successful Ford Dealerships in Central Florida.

Another personal story of self-reliance and self-determination is the story of Darrell Warner. As I sat in the Warner home, I asked how important self-reliance is in learning and growing. He responded, saying, "Do you have a Knowing Mind or a Learning Mind?" His answer caused me to pause and deeply consider what he meant.

I asked him to explain the Learning Mind.

"The Learning Mind is always striving to seek and know more. I would like to challenge that and say that in order to grow, we must have a Learning Mind; we must always be seeking to grow no matter where we are in our lives. We must be looking to obtain knowledge and develop expertise that will present us as the best in the world in our chosen professions. That is the position of operating from the state of a Learning Mind," he said.

As I left Mr. Warner's League City, Texas, home, I explored the concept of a Knowing Mind vs. a Learning Mind. If we would work to employ a Learning Mind in all that we do, we will have the motivation and spirit to learn and seek more. The Learning Mind is thus the fuel or the motivation that can help us to move to a higher level.

As I think of some of the Southern Greats who employ their Learning Mind as a tool of motivation, I think of Dr. Kent Smith, PhD., who also challenged the status quo and through self-reliance and determination became one of the youngest university presidents.

On an August afternoon in Langston, Oklahoma where it was well over 110 degrees, Dr. Smith was calm and cool as he fielded requests from different people. I had the opportunity to sit for a moment and interview him. I asked the relative new President of Langston University about the need to continually grow and develop oneself professionally and personally. He shared with me his role as not only President but also professor. (Dr. Smith still teaches classes along with all of his other duties.)

"By being in the classroom, I am not only influencing our students, but I am learning from them as well. I am continually being challenged and renewed," he said.

This experience and closeness to his students has already translated into his popularity among the student body and it does not hurt that he's in his early 40s either.

Dr. Smith also shared with me that he takes one day a week to purposely seek and work on the continuously evolving vision of Langston University. That is a spirit of a Learning Mind, continuously seeking ways to improve and to ensure that Langston is available to serve students in the years to come. This attitude of allowing the Learning Mind to motivate him has help Dr. Smith and his team to have record enrollment over the past two freshman classes.

I challenge you employ a Learning Mind on a daily basis and in all situations.

Greg Foster modeled self-reliance and determination when he was literally thrown into an unknown land with an unknown language, but he refused to let it hinder him.

A far cry and a long distance from Natchitoches, Louisiana, is Paris, France. At the time of our interview, Mr. Foster was a Major Project Manager with ExxonMobil, having the responsibility of managing the accounting on a major project. Although Mr. Foster was not required to speak French, he chose to learn it because being fluent in French would prove extremely beneficial. To do so, he committed up to twenty hours a week to master the French language. This time commitment was on top of his regular duties and responsibilities as a project manager.

I asked Mr. Foster how it paid off.

"We were in one of the first meetings with the entire team, and they assumed that I did not understand French. Let's say that they stated things that may have been better left unsaid. When I replied to their statement in French, the looks on their faces were priceless," he said.

Mr. Foster's determination and reliance on himself and not others to translate the French language for him earned him the respect of his colleagues. Transitioning to a new position in a job or moving to another country and learning another language are all experiences that require strong self-reliance and determination. You must believe that, in the end, you have the ability to achieve great success.

Bernice Washington and Clarence "CJ" Bland both had the ability to achieve great success and the self-motivation to see it come to pass. As I sat in the home of Bernice and Lt. Colonel Lyman Washington, I asked Mrs. Washington when she would retire. She said, "Never, I will continue to work, volunteer, and have fun." A former director with Bayer, after Mrs. Washington had retired she was searching for what her next step would be. This was when the opportunity to be a national speaker landed in her lap. Even though public speaking opportunities found her, she had to prepare and train to become an excellent speaker.

Her determination took her to the National Speakers' Association and she now delivers speeches and conducts trainings all over the world to all type of audiences.

Imagine converting a local newsletter into an electronic portal and top communication tool for many minority professionals. That's exactly what Mr. Bland did after burning a lot of midnight oil learning and teaching himself about the Internet and what would be the best way to market and position this new product and tool. Mr. Bland said, "It was critical that I continue to ask others about how and where we should grow the Minority Professional Network. I had to learn a lot about the technical side, but I also had to network a lot and learn about the business side of the Internet. This was critical in order to turn my contacts into contracts."

From difficult beginnings, Mr. Bland was able to start his business in fourteen markets and grow it to more than 200 markets for his site, www. MPNSITE.com.

Sometimes motivation is just as simple as doing your job. This is how it was for General Russell Honore', the United State Army General who was responsible for restoring the chaos of the aftermath of Hurricane Katrina in New Orleans. At the time of the storm, General Honore' was the commanding officer for 1st Division of Army and was responsible for the state of Mississippi. General Honore' and his team struggled to decide if they would go in before the storm or after. They decided to wait until after Hurricane Katrina had hit the Mississippi Gulf Coast before they would leave Atlanta. The General and his convoy left Atlanta on at 3 o'clock Tuesday morning and arrived at Camp Shelby Wiggin, Mississippi, at 10AM to ten troops waiting to go Iraq.

You must realize that the area around Camp Shelby had been devastated by Hurricane Katrina. I ask General Honore' what did he tell the troops.

"Get this place back in order," he said.
General Honore' would spend the rest of the day accessing damage and positioning troops to get Mississippi back in order. That evening he was part of conference call with his superiors and President George W. Bush. During this call, he was asked why was he in Mississippi because he had not received orders to go and he said, "I don't need anybody to tell me to do my job."

Think about how important that is for a moment.

Sometimes our motivation is that we must simply *just DO our job*.

The story does not end here.

Because General Honore' chose to *just do his job*, he would be called to restore the chaos in New Orleans caused by flooding throughout the city. New Orleans was under great unrest and in utter chaos. The general who had command over New Orleans and Louisiana had chosen to stay at his command post in San Antonio, Texas, instead of positioning himself in the hurricane's path. Due to the damage caused by Hurricane Katrina, he was unable to come into New Orleans. Because General Honore' had chosen to *just do his job*, he was in position to help New Orleans and his home state of Louisiana.

I asked General Honore' what was one of the major lessons that he learned going in New Orleans, and the General said, "There was a fear being portrayed by the media. People feared the poor. People were not looting; they were surviving." The General would explain that his motivation was to help these people who were his people. They were tired, cold, and hungry. His job was to let them know it was going to be all right and then to make it better.

As I listened to General Honore', I realized how important it is for us to *Just Do Our Job*. When we *Just Do Our Job*, we are placed in position to receive opportunities that may not currently exist or that may be unknown to us.

There are so many other stories I could share with you of the successes of the many individuals whose self-motivation led them to choose determination and self-reliance, and they have all had great success because of it.

REFLECTIONS FROM THE BLUFF:

What are three things from the past you can draw upon to provide you motivation?

1. _____

2. _____

3. _____

What are some hurdles/barriers that cause you to get stuck and become unmotivated?

_____

How can you use a Learning Mind to make a difference in your situation?

_____

Enjoying the Journey... Not Just the Destination

Journey *is defined as an act or instance of traveling from one place to another*

Destination *is defined as the final purpose or place.*

We are all familiar with a journey being the physical process of traveling from one place to another, as if going on a trip. However, a journey does not only require movement in the literal sense, moving oneself from point A to point B as in taking a trip to your favorite city or location. Oftentimes, a journey is a passage or progress through one stage and into the next. This stage can be about overcoming a fear, transitioning stages as we pursue new goals, a new job, or new opportunities. Whatever the process of traveling or the passage, the journey and not the destination should be the focus. On the journey is where we learn, grow, and even conquer many things in our lives.

In life, we often spend more time working <u>to</u> our destinations versus the amount of time we spend living at and enjoying the actual journey. It is this journey where we spend our time and where growth truly happens.

I have often heard of people speaking of the importance of enjoying the journey and not just focusing on the destination. It wasn't until recently that I focused on this statement and had an understanding of what this meant. I was challenged to reflect on my own life and realized that I was often focusing on what was next and not truly enjoying my journey or not even enjoying my current location.

When I look back at my life and the journey I am taking, I am reminded of my father. He loved building things. When I was a little boy, my father worked as a building contractor. He was always busy, working long hours. Yet, he was happy. During the late '70s, the economy shrunk and the housing market went flat. As a result, my dad had to get a job as a schoolteacher. Because he was a graduate of Mississippi Valley State University, he was able to teach building trades at the local vocational school. Even though he was making a living doing what he had to do to provide for us, he was not fully happy; and he definitely was not enjoying that journey. He began to slowly get back into building contracting and doing electrical and plumbing work in the evenings and weekends. It seemed as if he enjoyed the evening and weekends more than he did his day job. It is now clear to me that when he was following his passion and true calling as a builder, plumber, or electrician, he took pride in the journey.

As I write this passage, my dad is most likely somewhere doing what he enjoys: building, plumbing, or electrical work—or some combination of them. At the age of 73, he routinely works three to five days per week. Now, this is not because he has to, but because he loves what he does. During the other days of the week, he is playing golf or traveling with my mom. His life is truly an example to me of what enjoying the journey means.

As I sat and talked with many of the Southern Greats, they often talked about their journey and everything they encountered along the way. All of them learned to enjoy their journey. One the Southern Greats who first come to mind is **Dr. Emmitt Bashful,** the first Chancellor of Southern University of New Orleans. If you have ever had the opportunity to speak with Dr. Bashful, you would immediately realize the passion and purpose that he had to possess in order to accept the position to serve as chancellor.

Southern University of New Orleans was founded in 1953, a time when education opportunities for the Black working class were limited. Dr. Bashful saw it as his personal mission to provide any individual who wanted to improve their life an opportunity to do such. He shared many stories with me of the individuals SUNO helped, and consequently, how those lives were changed by being able to attend the university. Dr. Bashful chose the journey he was on to change the lives of impressionable students and give them opportunities they would not normally have. And he chose to enjoy his journey.

Milton Scott is someone who knows about the importance of continuing in the journey in order to see its benefits. Mr. Scott credited the art of juggling when he spoke with me about what motivated him to keep going on journey. He shared with me that in order to be effective during the journey, you must be able to juggle taking calculated risks and managing people. These skills will help you to be highly successful. Mr. Scott truly learned how to manage risk and people when he became the Chief Administrative Officer at Dynegy, a Fortune 500 company at the time. As Chief Administrative Officer, he headed several areas: risk management and credit, corporate planning, compliance and internal audit, insurance, human resources, global facilities management, corporate security, supply chain management, and was liaison to the board of directors. "It was a fast-paced, entrepreneurial company that Chuck Watson, CEO, had grown from scratch to a Fortune 500," Mr. Scott said. "There were not a lot of processes and controls, and it was a very close-knit group that had been together for a long time. I was an outsider; but I love challenges."

Very few people are good at both. His journey at Dynegy proved to be challenging, however, he chose to see value in his journey and appreciate it along the way.

Dexter Henderson's journey may have seemed boring and uneventful, but he knew that he needed to be faithful in it because it would eventually lead to more. He chose to look beyond his current job and current situation. As I sat down with Mr. Henderson, he talked about one of his assignments in the Middle East and Africa. While there, he was responsible for starting up a new division for IBM. He would routinely look at each country as its own startup and manage it accordingly. This kept him from getting bored or fatigued as he visited more than forty countries in thirty-six months in his position as the top representative for IBM. While he was traveling through all of these countries, Mr. Henderson was living across Windsor Lake from the Queen of England. He visited countries throughout Africa and the Middle East helping them develop and create new information technology infrastructures. He had the opportunity to meet iconic leaders including Bishop Desmond Tutu and former South Africa President Nelson Mandela. Mr. Henderson's journey took him to various, and sometimes remote, countries of the world and allowed him to have once-in-a-lifetime experiences. As he faithfully continued to do his job and travel to various countries, he found that he really did enjoy his journey.

When you are in the midst of your journey, grinding day after day, it may seem hard to remember to enjoy the journey. **Derrick Warren** knows firsthand the importance of remembering to enjoy the journey and valuing the process. "Always be part of the solution and not the problem," he said. I asked him how thinking this way helps him to focus on enjoying the journey and not focusing only on the destination. He said when he focuses on the solution; he is always working to make where he is better and not just trying to get to the next location. This always helps him remember to try to be better today than he was yesterday.

Dr. Kent Smith and Dr. Leonard Haynes are two Southern Greats who know about the importance of putting in the effort during the journey because they have seen the results when they finally reach their destination. Dr. Smith, president of Langston University, has always had three jobs. While in school at Southern University, he worked at Cohn Turner Fine Men's Clothier. I always remember him wearing great suits. Then, while he was earning his advanced degrees at Colorado State University, he used his experience at Cohn Turner to work at a local clothier. This job afforded him the opportunity to meet many members of administration that he otherwise would not have meet. While at Ohio University he was the Vice Chancellor of Student Affairs, but he often would take on other responsibilities to learn various aspects of the university operations. Being this involved and committed prepared him for his current job as President of Langston University. Even as President of Langston he still teaches in the classroom. Dr. Smith has said, "You must enjoy what you do. Your next opportunities will come from the relationships that you develop and build." This statement made me think about how important it is to enjoy where you are while still being prepared for what the future will bring.

Dr. Haynes has also put in great effort so that he can enjoy his journey. As I sat in the corner office on K Street in Washington DC interviewing Dr. Haynes, I had a feeling I had come full circle. You see, Dr. Haynes was one of my professors at Southern. He was a challenging and thought-provoking professor. He was the type of professor who would have you read a passage and then, in class, he'd challenge you to forget what you had read and explore the true meaning of the text. He'd challenge you to apply the passage to your life at that moment and your current situation.

When I asked Dr. Haynes what motivated him to keep going and enjoy the moment he said, "I look to make a positive contribution to society on a daily basis." As we continued to talk he shared that, "no matter how well you are doing, if your race doesn't have success then you are failing." As I plundered these two statements, I realized how important it is for us to be in the moment, truly enjoying our purpose and helping others during our journey and not after we arrive.

Because of the impact he made on everyone, Dr. Haynes' name often comes up when I speak with other Southern Greats including Bishop Joseph Walker and James Verrett. I asked Dr. Haynes why he continued to do the work that he does. He told me, "White, (Dr. Haynes always referred to us by our last name), everybody can do something to help society succeed. It is critical that we work to get as many people into the full system. This is one of the missions that our HBCUs serve and must continue to serve. At the end of each day, we must ask [ourselves] what positive contributions we made."

True to form, Dr. Haynes' response framed why it is important to enjoy your journey and not just focus on what is next. What contribution will you make today that will make this world a better place? What people will I help today? I challenge you to consider these two questions as you begin each day. I have personally found that as I ponder these two questions at the beginning of my days and weeks, I am profoundly more productive and happy.

Making the world a better place while enjoying each day of the journey is something Mrs. Bernice Washington can honestly say she is doing. Mrs. Washington is retired from Bayer and is in her golden years. However, based on her scheduled she is busier than ever and having fun. Mrs. Washington leads the BWJ Consulting Group, a training and consulting company that helps people reach their maximum potential. When you see Mrs. Washington in front of people you will realize that she truly is enjoying her journey. I asked Mrs. Washington when will she retire and she said, "I will be working to help others until I am physically unable; whatever direction this takes me I am unsure, however I plan to enjoy the ride." As Board member of the Dallas Fort Worth Airport Authority and Chairwoman of the Presbyterian Hospital Board, Mrs. Washington is definitely not slowing down her ride. Currently that vehicle is going 100 miles per hour and she is doing the driving.

The great life examples lived out by many Southern Greats have not gone unnoticed. Their journeys help to teach all of us the importance of appreciating the lessons learned and the positive experiences while on the journey. One person who has set this example is General Russel Honore'. I had the pleasure of interviewing the General and asked him how and why he has enjoyed such a long career in the U.S. Army. General Honore' talked with me about all of the young men and women that he has been able to help along the way.

While he attended Southern University, he was often given "DO OVERS" and the professors ensured that he was well-abled, prepared, and fully equipped when he graduated. When he became an officer in the US Army, he often found himself with new soldiers who were not totally ready for the work ahead and would need more than one opportunity to get it right. He would extend to them a "DO OVER." Being able to help others and fighting environmental injustices are the General's way of maintaining value in his journey and enjoying every minute of it.

Dr. Rani Whitfield also talks about his opportunity to enjoy his journey by being able to be of service to others as a medical doctor and health advocate. He's motivated to give back to the community. Even as I was interviewing him on a Sunday afternoon, Dr. Whitfield was busy doing volunteer physicals for a local community college's women's basketball team. When asked why he does it, he said, "I have been blessed and I must do what I can to help others. We [should] always be looking forward to helping others." Dr. Whitfield has found a way to blend his two loves of medicine and music and truly enjoy his journey. See, as Da' Hip Hop Doc, Dr. Whitfield is able to educate and entertain youth and adults about the importance of a healthy lifestyle.

"I was on stage speaking to some kids and decided to bus an old Eric B and Rakeem rap. The kids began to listen and enjoy. From that point, I realized that I could mix music and medicine, so I started to developing raps to convey the message of medicine." Da' Hip Doc was born because Dr. Whitfield was enjoying the journey of sharing health strategies with others and new opportunities were created for him. He is able to travel the world, take the microphone, enter the stage, and truly connect with our youth about the dangers of AIDS and many preventable diseases.

I challenge you to seek ways to mix your passions and purpose along your personal journey. Seek to mix these two Ps, so that new opportunities are born. These opportunities were often right beside us. But because you are willing to take a different view, a different look and truly enjoy your journey, you now see the same things in a different light and with a different perspective. This new perspective will often lead to new beginnings and new opportunities.

As Vice President with Boeing Space Division, Darrell Warner also knows the importance of focusing on the journey. He offered this advice: "No job is too small or too little to do your best. So, in every job you must always give your best effort." Warner also continued to share that in order for you to always give your best efforts, you must enjoy where you are and what you are doing. I would challenge you to determine what you can learn and what can you add to each and every situation that you are facing today. This will prove that your journey is not only about you, but it is also about those around you who are helping you along the way and those who will learn from your example.

As we sat in the basement of Vincent Scott Lyons' home, I saw that it was the people of his organization who excited and fueled him along his journey. Vincent talked about how as the president of a major division of a Fortune 500 company he was able to positively impact the lives of the many people who were part of his team. Being able to help people grow and actually see their growth is one of the things that excites him along his journey.

Now, don't get me wrong, the destination is indeed important. However, the destination will never be appreciated and valued, if you do not enjoy and value the journey as it takes you there.

Arthur George shifted positions in his chair as he begin to frame his answer to "what is the importance of sticking with your values?". He shared an example of when he was working with one of Texas Instrument's largest clients. Mr. George had suggested several recommendations to the client that he felt were in the client's best interest. However, the client did not receive it that way and did not want to hear from Mr. George. Nonetheless, he stuck to his recommendations. Next, this client's CEO called the Texas Instruments' CEO and demanded that Mr. George be fired. This critical moment in his career taught Mr. George the importance of focusing on what is right and what is in the best interest of your client. As I listen to him, I also realized how important it is to enjoy what you are doing and be comfortable with where you are in your journey in order to appreciate the destination.

MINOR TO MAJOR

When you talk about enjoying the journey, I would be totally remised if I did not share the story of **Trenidad Hubbard**. Mr. Hubbard grew up on the South Side of Chicago and always had the dream and goal of playing major league baseball. See, his journey was not that of a high school prodigy who received the multi-million dollar contract. His journey would take him through Southern University where he met his wife, Angela, and where he met a second father, Coach Roger Cador. As a team captain for Southern's baseball team, Mr. Hubbard was required to witness try-outs of the new players. During these try-outs, he would watch Coach Cador's reactions to bad players.

"(Coach) was not going to crush the player's dream. He was not going to deny him the opportunity," he said. Mr. Hubbard used that attitude as he pursued his dream of being a major league baseball player. In 1986, he was drafted by the Houston Astros and it was not until 1994 that he made his major league debut. That was eight years of being a journeyman in the minor league. When I asked him how did he stick it out, he said, "I enjoyed playing baseball." The love and desire of enjoying the moment is what allowed him to enjoy an additional nine years in the Major Leagues to play baseball until he was 39 years old.

Even today, Mr. Hubbard's daily work is around baseball and he is enjoying the journey.

In order to enjoy the journey, you must be actively following your passion and operating in your purpose. The journey is the ride we endure to reach our destination. The funny and perhaps most compelling part to enjoying your journey is that when you are truly spending time in your purpose you don't have time to look down the road toward your endpoint, you have to focus on the moment, the now, the present state of your journey.

When I asked these Southern Greats about their journey, they all reminded me that it is full of twists and turns; that often each turn would bring about unknown and new challenges which will strengthen you and help you to reach your next peak and a new destination.

REFLECTIONS FROM THE BLUFF:

Take a moment to write down at least one long term personal goal (your destination):

_____
_____
_____
_____
_____
_____

Visualize and write some of the peaks that you will enjoy and how you will enjoy:

_____
_____
_____
_____
_____
_____

Think about and write some of the valleys that you may experience. Share how you will overcome at least one of these valleys:

_____
_____
_____
_____

_____

_____

_____

_____

Reflect back to past unplanned and unexpected occurrences in your life that assisted you in growing into a stronger and better person:

_____

_____

_____

_____

_____

_____

_____

ALWAYS BRING VALUE

How is value defined? Oftentimes when you think of the word value, you think of strong excellence and merit. Something or someone of value is said to be useful and regarded with high esteem. A relationship can be valued for its usefulness, or an individual valued for their wisdom. With that said, in order for someone to be valued, they must in turn bring value to the forefront.

"Always Bring Value" is a phrase—from my grandfather—that has resonated with me since I was a child. I was blessed to grow up less than two miles from my paternal grandfather, John Allen White, in Prentiss, Mississippi. All of us grandkids would refer to him as Daddy John. Prentiss is a small town with two small, segregated high schools. Even in the '70s and '80s, you could feel and sense the racial tension that existed. With this type of racial tension, it was obvious that an individual's value was stripped from them and they were minimized to just the color of their skin. My grandfather, John Allen, was the person who taught us that based on what you give out, you would most certainly be paid in return for your true value far beyond just the color of your skin.

Daddy John was born in 1906 and had to quit school while he was in elementary school to help support his family. Even though he had very little formal education, he was a man of great wisdom. He often taught me that in order to make it, I would have to give people more than they expected. This was the first of many lessons I would learn from my grandfather about bringing value as an individual.

Daddy John was considered one of the best carpenters in the area. As a preteen and teenager, my Saturdays were spent working with Daddy John. Looking back, I realize that I was probably of little help to him but the time together for Daddy John was more about teaching me work ethic and value. I can remember numerous times when this man with a second grade education would look at a blank wall and design and build a beautiful set of kitchen cabinets around it. He often would build or create something nicer than the customer had originally requested or paid for. Daddy John would say, "I thought I would give you a little something extra." He was always working to bring value to the situation. Watching him taught me that always bringing value meant that you were bringing something of worth, something of excellence, to another individual, to a situation, or to your job. You are valued for what you bring not who you are.

Like my grandfather, these Southern Greats were deliberate in their profession, intentionally and consistently bringing value to their jobs. For example, take Dexter Henderson, a Vice President with IBM. On his first assignment at IBM in Research Triangle Park, North Carolina, Mr. Henderson would routinely work the second shift everyday, without pay, in order to learn how the their team's software was being utilized in production. His day consisted of working up to ten hours designing software, and he then would work another entire shift on the manufacturing floor. His friends and coworkers would often tell him that he was crazy for giving IBM those extra hours. But Dexter knew that he was doing it for a purpose. The extra hours he worked allowed him to bring value to the company because of his knowledge of the ins and outs of the software program. He was also bringing value to himself through his diligence and hard work.

Mr. Henderson likened the extra work to a football practice. He called it, "running the sprints after practice". As a football player, you almost always have extra sprints after a tough practice. The coach does this so that you can bring that extra value during the game—during the time it counts. When he had a meeting with senior management, it was game time for Mr. Henderson. It turned out that his

IBM facility was having problems with the design and manufacturing integration of a product. This is a technical way of saying that their design was not working on the production floor. This was where the extra time and effort that he had put in would enable him to understand the problems with the design software and correct them. It was in this meeting that Mr. Henderson was able to bring value to IBM.

"I was invited to the meeting and had to stand on the wall. I first wondered if I was supposed to be there because I didn't even have a seat at the table. As the Vice-President began to discuss the problem no one could offer any solutions. After about an hour, I raised my hand and said I knew what the answer was. At the time, I still had a heavy New Orleans accent so everyone in the room was looking at me wondering who I was. I, then, began to explain the problem and the solution to correct the problem. As the meeting was closing, the Vice-President asked me to go his his office to discuss it further," he said.

By doing those extra sprints, working longer hours, and always providing more, Mr. Henderson's career skyrocketed through the ranks of IBM. Always bringing value earned him the position of manager in four years which normally takes six to ten years to accomplish. Today, Mr. Henderson is responsible for multi-billion dollar company.

Milton Scott has been very successful as the Chief Administrative Officer for Dynegy. He has had to work hard and bring great value to a variety of situations within the company in order to be as successful as he has over the past 30 years. During our interview, I asked Mr. Scott what were the memorable incidences when he had to bring value to the company. He immediately thought of the near merger of Dynegy and Enron.

Back in 2001, the plan was to keep the potential acquisition quiet from anyone outside of the company because of the enormity of this kind of business venture. Mr. Scott fully utilized his skills to try and make the deal happen.

When it was time for Scott and his team at Dynegy to meet with Enron, they discovered that Enron was not who they said they were. It was later revealed that Enron was at the center of a huge scandal involving billions of dollars that the company hid from its board of directors, investors, and the Securities and Exchange Commission. This resulted in Enron filing for bankruptcy.

Needless to say, there was no deal for Dynegy to purchase Enron. Nonetheless, Mr. Scott learned a valuable lesson from this experience.

"No matter what the value is, you must do the due diligence," he said and his due diligence brought value to his company and his team.

Bringing value also means that your work ethic must be intrinsically motivated. You must be willing to work hard no matter what. Working hard is a core value that Greg Baranco strongly believes in.

Let's step back in time to the early '70s . During this time, the racial landscape in Baton Rouge, Louisiana, was tense. At this time, Baranco was a young man in his early twenties, and he wanted to be a car salesman. Even though Mr. Baranco was one of the students who integrated the local Catholic High School, attended Tulane, and had interned at a Fortune 500 automobile manufacturer, the car dealership did not want to allow him the opportunity to be a new car salesman solely based on the color of his skin. He did not let up. As a result, his persistence convinced the manager to give him a three-month trial at the dealership. He chose not to allow his skin color to be a factor, but rather to focus on how he could add value to the dealership during his trial period.

"Those three months taught me how little I did know about the car industry; however I knew that I could outwork anyone," he said.

Because of his diligence and work ethic, the top salesman to the general manager took Mr. Baranco under his wings, mentored him, and helped him be successful. Because of this relationship, Mr. Baranco became a fulltime salesman and eventually the General Manager of the dealership. He did not allow his race to be barrier when dealing with customers. Ironically, Mr. Baranco sold a Ford Pinto to David Duke, former grand wizard of the Klu Klux Klan.

I asked Mr. Baranco what propelled him to General Manager and he said that as a salesman he realized he needed to know the various areas of the car business. Knowing how the finance division worked would help him get deals done and knowing how the service department worked would help him keep customers satisfied, he said. This strategy helped strengthen in him the importance of continuously learning and adding value to his current situation.

Mr. Baranco believes that you should never be guilty of saying "this is not my job" or "this is not my responsibility." Instead, you should seek out ways that you can bring value to the company, then work hard at getting things done.

My next interview led me to the Birmingham Civil Rights Institute to meet with Southern Great **Dr. Lawrence Pijeaux**. During our interview, I made the mistake of referring to the Institute as a museum and Dr. Pijeaux quickly corrected me by saying that the Birmingham Civil Rights Institute is not a museum first, but it is an educational institution that provides valuable information to hundreds of thousands of people yearly.

The value that Dr. Pijeaux has brought to the institute is evident by the advancements that have happened since he became the director. In 2005, Dr. Pijeaux led the Institute to accreditation as a history museum from the American Association of Museums. Following this, the Institute was named Attraction of the Year in 2009; and most recently the Institute has been named an affiliate of the Smithsonian Institute. There are only 115 museums as affiliates of the Smithsonian Institute out of 17,000 possible.

The value that Dr. Pijeaux brings to the Institute is evidenced by some of the awards that he has received over the years for his work. These awards are a testament to what he has achieved by working for the Birmingham Civil Rights Institute. Some of the awards under his leadership include: two consecutive national awards presented at the White House by then First Lady Laura Bush for community service—the Coming Up Taller Award in 2007 and the inaugural National Medal for Museum Service in 2008. In 2006, Pijeaux was named Alabama Tourism Executive of the Year. His accomplishments show us that adding value to your surroundings, no matter where you are, will in turn add great value to you and those around you. A person who realizes, commits, and adds value to the situation and more importantly to team is the definition of a leader.

"I always wanted to be the best engineer when I was an engineer; when I was a manager I always wanted to be the best manager; when I became a leader, I wanted to be the best leader that I could be. I always made it known that

I wanted to pursue the tough problems that could not be solved. I was always putting my reputation on the line; however, it allowed me to always bring value to our team," said Elliot Lyons when I asked him how important it is for someone to add value to any experience in their lives.

The truth is we are all blessed to be able to bring value to our relationships and jobs. When we understand the importance of bringing value, we will choose to be a leader. Being the proverbial educator and teacher, Dr. Haynes challenged me to share the following steps: **THE FIVE Fs OF ADDING VALUE**

FOCUS – minimize the distractions be in the moment.

FAITH - have faith in your capabilities. You must say, "I believe in myself."

FOLLOW UP – on what you have you have chosen to start.

FOLLOW THROUGH – make sure tasks are being done.

FINISH – complete all tasks.

As I left Dr. Haynes' office in downtown Washington DC, I could not stop thinking about how employing these Five Fs in any situation would add value. Think about where you are today and the projects or tasks that you have in front of you. How would employing the Five Fs help you to be valuable, do more, and be more?

As I ask **Attorney Claire Babineaux-Fontenot**, Executive Vice President and Treasurer of Wal-Mart Stores, Inc., about always adding value, she said key question that we should ask is, "why was I placed here?" She believes we are placed in every situation to add value. She would explain that this starts with being humble and accepting that you don't need to be everything, know everything, or have everything to be of value. By being humble and sincerely seeking why your are placed in a particular situation will cause you to think and reflect.

I asked Mrs. Babineaux-Fontenot how she applies this principle to her leadership style and to being successful in her career. She said, "my leadership style is Gap Leadership." This was my first time hearing someone refer to their style of leadership as Gap Leadership. So, I had to ask her what did she mean. She would explain that as a leader it was her job to fill in the "gaps" of her team. She did not necessarily have to be the smartest or the hardest worker (this does not me she is not smart or does not work hard) on her team. She simply has to add value by filling in those gaps.

"My job is to sing the notes that others don't sing. As the leader, I am not required to sing the chorus. I must sing the notes that no one else will sing," she said. In order to be valuable to and for our team, as a leader, we must be willing and prepared to do what they rest cannot and will not do.

When I ask Pamela Whitley, a senior executive with the Federal Aviation Administration, how she has been able to add value to her team and FFA. She gave me three things that she employs in every situation. They are:

1. Be the best at your job. Don't be average. You must continuously strive to be the best at what you do and do it better than anyone else.
2. Understand the work environment. You must understand the business, the people, and the politics.
3. Understand the money and how do you get paid. No matter where you work that job is driven by a budget and you must understand how and where the money comes from.

When Ms. Whitley mastered these three steps, she was considered valuable whether it was her first job with the Tennessee Valley Authority as an engineer responsible for twenty-eight men or in her current position as an executive with the FAA, where she is responsible for working with the international community to ensure flight standards and to lead the development of new aviation technology.

Elliot Jerome Lyons, would share with me that in order to add value, "One must be very comfortable in being the absolute best in what they are doing and you must seek to be the best where you are." This principal and concept would often lead Mr. Lyons to ask for the tough and seemingly impossible assignments. "If no one else can solve it give to me," is his motto. This along with a lot hard work has made him very valuable to General Motors, United Technologies, Leggett and Platt, and Navistar.

As I close out this chapter, I believe that it is important to note that no matter where you are or what situation you may be in, we must seek to understand why we were placed there. Then, determine what you can do differently to make a difference. Oftentimes what we can do differently is not easily determined. We sometimes have to seek advice and help from others to fully understand why we have been placed into a particular situation and what can be done differently to add value. We must be willing to always work hard and help others.

REFLECTIONS FROM THE BLUFF:
What are three skills that others see as valuable and briefly describe how you use these skills:

_____
_____
_____
_____
_____
_____
_____
_____
_____

List at least one way you can utilize one of these skills immediately in your current job or business:

_____
_____
_____
_____
_____
_____
_____
_____

How will you utilize the Five Fs given by Southern Great Dr. Leonard Haynes?

Focus:_____
_____
_____

Faith:_____
_____
_____

Follow-up:_____
_____
_____

Follow-through:_____
_____
_____

Finish:_____
_____
_____

Conclusion

Over the past 130 plus years, Southern University has had the mission and purpose of truly meeting students were they are and propelling them on the path to greatness. It was my pleasure to meet, listen to, and learn from just a fraction of the "Greats" who have matriculated through Southern University and A&M College.

Hopefully this book has challenged you to look at yourself and identify your own greatness. It will help you to strive for more, seek more, and be more. If you attend Southern University this is what you will be challenged to do by your professors, peers, and administrators.

I must also say thanks to all of those individuals who gave of their time to be part of this project. You did not have this to do but you saw and heard the vision that was given to me.

It is my personal mission and goal to **H**elp **O**thers **W**in **A**nd **R**ealize **D**reams. Until the next installment, I challenge you to continue to DREAM and WIN.

HOWARD

SOUTHERN GREATS INTERVIEWED

Attorney Claire Babineaux-Fontenot- Sr. Vice President and Treasurer of Wal-Mart Stores, Inc.

Greg Baranco – Owner of Baranco Automotive Group (Mercedes of Buckhead)

C.J. Bland – Founder of minorityprofessionalnetwork.com

Lou Brock – Hall of Fame baseball player and minister at Abundant Life Fellowship Church in St. Charles, Missouri

Dennis S. Brown - President and CEO of Destiny Investments

Darrel Carmen, MD – Partner at Georgia Urology

Felicia Coney – Executive with Procter and Gamble

Kelvin Coney – Executive with Procter and Gamble

Lavell Crump – aka David Banner, rapper, record producer and actor.

Samuel Davis Jr. – CEO of Gas and Water Company

Rev. Ken Ellis- Retired NFL Player and Assistant Pastor

Attorney Cleo Fields- Attorney and former US Congressman

Greg Foster- Retired ExxonMobil executive

Art George – Retired executive and motivational speaker

Rev. Ladell Graham – Retired investment banker and pastor of The Champion Center, Richmond, TX.

Jeniffer Harper Taylor - President of the Siemens Foundation

Leonard Haynes, Ph.D. – Senior Executive with United States Government

Dexter Henderson - Vice President and business line executive, IBM Power Systems

General Russel Honore – Retired US Army General and environmental activist

Trenidad Hubbard – 18-year veteran of major league baseball

Vincent Lyons – Corporate executive of Fortune 500 Company

Elliott J. Lyons - Corporate executive of Fortune 500 Company

Irving Matthews - Founder and CEO of Matthews Automotive Group

Lawrence J. Pijeaux, Ph.D. - president and CEO of the Birmingham Civil Rights Institute

Rev. Leslie Smith – Founder and CEO of Change Happens!,

Milton Scott - Chairman and CEO of The Tagos Group

Bernice Washington- President and CEO of BJW Consulting Group, LLC

James Verrett – National TV Sportscaster

Maurice Sholas, MD – Founder of Sholas Medical Consulting

Rev. Byron Stevenson – Founding Pastor of Fort Bend Church of Sugarland, TX

Kent Smith, Ph.D. – 16th President of Langston University

Joseph Stewart – Retired Vice President with Kellogg

Thomas Todd- Attorney and civil rights activists

Warren Valdry, Ph.D. – President of Valdry and Associates

Bishop Joseph Walker – International Presiding Bishop-Elect of the Full Gospel Baptist Church

Rev. Aeneas Williams – NFL Hall of Fame Player and pastor of Spirit of the Lord Family Church, St. Louis, MO
Rani Whitfield, MD – Physician and International Medical Spokesman
Bruce Walker - Owner of Rehabilitation Hospital
Darrell Warner – Vice President at Space Division Boeing
Pamela Whitley – Sr. Executive with FFA

Deceased
Emmitt Bashful, Ph.D. – Founding Chancellor of Southern University New Orleans
Isaac Greggs, Ph.D. – Former band director of Southern University and A&M College
James Freemont, MD – Physician and medical director
Jewel Prestage, Ph.D. – First Black female to earn a doctorate in public policy
Donald C. Wade – Former Southern University alumni director

ABOUT THE AUTHORS

Howard White is a native of Prentiss, Mississippi, and a 1989 mechanical engineering graduate of Southern University and A&M College. During his time at Southern he served as a member of the Southern University Board of Supervisors, SGA President, Alpha Phi Alpha Fraternity, Inc. and various other organizations.

After graduation, Howard worked for two Fortune 500 companies, DuPont and Nalco Chemical, in a variety of sales and marketing roles. The roles ranged from regional marketing responsibilities for new start-up products in the environment arena to direct sales responsibilities in the food and beverage and light industrial markets. Through hard work and creative ideas, he was able to be consistently rank as top salesman. Howard was national salesman of the year out of 300 salesmen.

In 1999, Howard left Corporate America and started a retail store that specializes in collegiate apparel. By utilizing creative ideas and marketing programs, he positioned Top Choice Products as market leader in Southern University merchandise.

In 2007, Howard expanded into the promotional marketing arena. Since this time TOP Choice has been able to work with more than twenty Fortune 500 companies, various regional companies, and a host small businesses. TOP Choice not only provides its clients with product, they provide innovative programs, creative ideas, and simple solutions.

Recently, Howard has joined the John Maxwell Team (JMT) as a certified leadership, Coach, Trainer and Speaker. As a JMT member, Howard trains outside organizations and companies on leadership and marketing. This also helps Howard bring enhanced leadership practices to his organizations that he belongs to.

When not working, Howard enjoys spending time with his wife, Janice, participating in baseball with their son, Howard III, and playing golf. Howard is also active in his church, Living Faith Christian Center, 100 Black Men, Southern University Alumni Association, and Alpha Phi Alpha Fraternity, Inc.

Howard's first book, *TOP Secrets To Creating a TOP Performing Business*, can be purchased directly from www.teamtopchoice.com or from Amazon.com.

Candace J. Semien is a native of Baton Rouge, Louisiana, and a 1994 print journalism graduate of Southern University and A&M College. She has twenty years of journalistic, scientific, and technical writing, copyediting, and publishing experience. She serves as managing editor and reporter for the Jozef Syndicate where she helps writers, photographers, and illustrators of all genres *record life and publish dreams*. Jozef's books are available at www.jozefsyndicate.com

HOWARD WHITE

www.ingramcontent.com/pod-product-compliance
Lightning Source LLC
Chambersburg PA
CBHW071923290426
44110CB00013B/1456